SPEAKING THE PAST

HERITAGE, DISCOURSE, AND PUBLISHING IN THE DIGITAL AGE

UNIVERSITY COLLEGE ROOSEVELT
MIDDELBURG, THE NETHERLANDS
23 - 24 OCTOBER 2019

Theran Press

Theran Press is the academic publishing imprint of Silver Goat Media.

Theran is dedicated to authentic partnerships with our academic associates, to the quality design of scholarly books, and to elite standards of peer review.

Theran seeks to free intellectuals from the confines of traditional publishing.

Theran scholars are authorities and revolutionaries in their respective fields.

Theran encourages new models for generating and distributing knowledge.

For our creatives, for our communities, for our world.

WWW.THERANPRESS.ORG

This book was designed and produced by Silver Goat Media, LLC. Fargo, ND U.S.A.
www.silvergoatmedia.com
SGM, the SGM goat, Theran Press, and the Theran theta are trademarks of Silver Goat Media.

Cover photograph: Helle Hochscheid
El-bowls made at the pre-conference workshop taught by Michael Strand.

Cover design: Jonathan Rutter © 2021 SGM
This book was typeset in Kings Caslon by Cady Ann Rutter.

ISBN-10: 1-944296-18-6
ISBN-13: 978-1-944296-18-6

A portion of the annual proceeds from the sale of this book is donated to the Longspur Prairie Fund.
www.longspurprairie.org

SPEAKING THE PAST

HERITAGE, DISCOURSE, AND
PUBLISHING IN THE DIGITAL AGE

EDITED BY HELLE HOCHSCHEID & PETER SCHULTZ

In memoriam
Mitchell R. McInnis (1973 - 2020)
mors immatura

Failing to fetch me at first keep encouraged,
Missing me one place search another,
I stop somewhere waiting for you.

- Walt Whitman

TABLE OF CONTENTS

CONTRIBUTORS

Núria Bofarull Manzano (BA, University College Roosevelt) studied photography and visual media in Barcelona before coming to the Netherlands, where she graduated with a degree in art history, sociology, and art & design. Thanks to the UCR Undergraduate Research Fund she conducted research at the Archives of Mauthausen Memorial (Vienna) and designed a curatorial proposal for the photographs of Francesc Boix that included the larger material culture of Mauthausen. She is currently applying to master's programs in the field of curating.

Ash Brown (BA, University College Roosevelt) has studied a diversity of subjects but focuses on psychology, archaeology, and ancient history. At first glance, these topics seem a strange combination, but to her/them they provide an interesting perspective on both ancient and current civilizations. Inspired by their experience working with Waterloo Uncovered, Ash is considering a master's in rehabilitation therapy and in the future would like to explore the ways in which archaeological excavation can offer a therapeutic connection with the past.

Michael Burke (PhD, University of Amsterdam) is Professor of Rhetoric at Utrecht University. He is the author of *Literary Reading, Cognition and Emotion: An Exploration of the Oceanic Mind* (Routledge, 2011). He is the former Honours Dean of Utrecht University (2016-2021) and a former President of the International Poetics and Linguistics Association (2010-2012). He has published extensively in the fields of rhetoric, reading, and stylistics. In 2021, he was a Visiting Scholar at the University of Cambridge (Homerton College).

Sien Christiaanse (BA, University College Roosevelt) studied antiquity and art history. Her research interests include critical heritage studies, the interpretation of material culture, and the experience of historic spaces. She is currently pursuing her studies at Trinity College Dublin with the M.Phil Public History and Cultural Heritage.

Julia Cottrell (BA, University College Roosevelt) has interests that include material culture, identity, and space. She has previously participated in a collaboration between the Koninklijk Zeeuwsch Genootschap der Wetenschappen, the University of Amsterdam, and UCR, tasked with 'bringing seventeenth-century maps to life'. Julia is currently a marketer in Rotterdam.

Laura du Pree (University College Roosevelt, 2021) is majoring in antiquity, art history, and philosophy. Her research interests are mainly ancient Greek philosophy and socially engaged contemporary art.

Clarissa Frascadore (BA, University College Roosevelt) is an art historian with a passion for history and antiquity. She is currently a master's student at Utrecht University where she is focusing on modern and contemporary art. Her research interests vary from ancient Greek art, to modernist and feminist art. She has worked on the bio-archaeological project of Phaleron in Athens (American School of Classical Studies).

Danielle Gravon (PhD, University of Mancester) is a map historian, artist, and conservationist. Her research investigates the relationship between sacred geographies, map making, and the Reformation image debates in the work of Gerhard Mercator. Danielle has held fellowships from the German-American Clubs Foundation, J.B. Harley Research Fellowship in the History of Cartography, and the Belgian American Educational Foundation.

Vicki Haverkate-Emmerson (MA, University College London) is an archaeologist and experienced educator. She is head of formal education at Waterloo Uncovered, a charity which combines archaeological research with supporting the physical or mental recovery of military personnel. Her research explores how difficult aspects of the past, such as conflict and colonialism, can be used to stimulate global citizenship and self-efficacy.

Laetitia Mizero Hellerud (MS, University of Mary) is an entrepreneur, author, and former Bush Foundation Fellow. She is the founder of UBUNTU Consulting, an intercultural firm specializing in creating equitable workplaces and communities. Her areas of interest include: strategic planning, change management, DEIJ, organization development, training and facilitation, and systems thinking. Laetitia's most recent book is *Turning Points: True Stories of Thriving Through Adversity* (UBUNTU Consulting, 2018).

Yolande Hobbs (BA, University College Roosevelt) is an honours graduate who majored in antiquity, rhetoric, and art history. Her main academic interests are in the niche fields of auction house theory and humorology. She is currently pursuing a master's in international business specialising in entrepreneurship and business development at Maastricht University and intends to open an auction house in the future.

Helle Hochscheid (PhD, University of Amsterdam) teaches antiquity and heritage at University College Roosevelt. She is co-founder of the Ancient Sculpture Association. Her research focuses on meanings and manufacture in ancient craft, in particular sculpture. She also takes an interest in the question of what modern societies need to retain of these skills to be sustainable for the future. Among her books are *Networks of Stone. Sculpture and Society in Archaic and Classical Athens* (Oxford, 2015) and *The Value of Making. Ancient Craft in Theory and Practice* (Brepols, in press 2021).

Léa Jörg (BA, University College Roosevelt) graduated with law and anthropology majors. Following her passion on the topics of social and environmental justice, she participated in the 'Cities of Refuge' research project, where she focused on local governments and the concept of 'urban citizenship' in Switzerland. Her liberal arts and sciences education reflects her interdisciplinary interests, which led her to engage in the course 'The Global Artefact'.

Marjolein Kik (University College Roosevelt, 2021) is a liberal arts and sciences student majoring in antiquity, history, and art history. Her research interests include the study, recreation, and representation of historical material culture, and what this can teach us about both historical and contemporary society. In Fall 2021 she is set to continue her studies at University College Dublin with the MSc Experimental Archaeology & Material Culture.

Anna Lee is a lifelong producer, creator, and educator. She has helped artists of all genres expand their creative endeavors for nearly twenty years. She is the Creative Director of Workerby (pronounced worker-bee), a company founded on the principles of structure, creativity, and the importance of every task required to make something happen (aka: doing the good work). Through her workshops, chakra portraits, and guidance sessions, one gains a better understanding of the individual, the collective, and their responsibility to the self and each other through creative exercises, contemplation, and discussion.

Taylor Lee (BA, University College Roosevelt) completed their bachelor in antiquity and history with a special interest in data science. They are particularly interested in how interdisciplinary approaches can provide better insight to people's past and heritage. Taylor hopes to pursue a career using methods from data science to make archaeology more accessible and informative through open access and predictive analysis.

Mike Lippman (PhD, Duke University) is an Associate Professor of Practice at the University of Nebraska Lincoln. He focuses his research and teaching on ancient Greek drama, particularly Aristophanes, but considers himself a generalist, also teaching large-lecture introductory, experiential courses on Sparta, Athens, and ancient athletics. He recently won the SCS Award for Teaching at the College Level (2018) as well as the CAMWS award for College Teaching (2021). He translated Aristophanes' *Knights* with Willie Major and is now working on a monograph project with Peter Schultz and David Gill tentatively entitled *Victorious Athens: Cleon, Pylos and the Twilight of Empire: 429-421 B.C.E.*

Artemisia Loesberg (University College Roosevelt, 2021) is an undergraduate antiquity student who has completed tracks in antiquity, rhetoric, and history. Her research interests include gender in the ancient world, magic in the ancient world, ancient Greek religion, and the cognitive science of religion. She is currently finishing her bachelor thesis, which focuses on perceptions of the female body in ancient Greece and the role of embodiment in worship.

Mitchell R. McInnis was an award-winning poet, writer, editor, traveler, and scholar. He was born and raised in Montana, USA. He was co-founder of the innovative arts journal *HoboEye*, now-retired. His poetry and criticism recently appeared in journals such as *The Southeast Review* and *The Collagist*, among numerous others. Mitch is also the author of the acclaimed poetry collection, *The Missing Shade of Blue* (Xlibris, 2004).

Nancy Mykoff (PhD, New York University) is faculty at University College Roosevelt. Her research and teaching privilege the lives of ordinary people. Recent publications look at girlhood through the lens of leisure, and transnational life writing. Courses explore histories of women and children, popular culture, race, ethnicity, and disability. Her current work explores Native lives.

Sanne Rossel (University College Roosevelt, 2021) is a liberal arts and sciences student majoring in antiquity, art history, and world religions. Her future plans include a course in restoration of stained glass, as well as a double master's in heritage management and applied archaeology.

Peter Schultz (PhD, University of Athens) is an archaeologist, entrepreneur, and conservationist. He is the current Executive Director of the Longspur Prairie Fund. Peter has held fellowships from the Fulbright Foundation, the A.G. Leventis Foundation, the ASCSA, among many others. His research interests include ancient Greek art, archaeological theory, and modern Greek poetry, music, feasting, and landscape. His most recent book, co-edited with Kristen Seaman, is *Artists and Artistic Production in Ancient Greece* (Cambridge University Press, 2017).

Emily Selove (PhD, UCLA) is Senior Lecturer in Medieval Arabic Language and Literature at the University of Exeter. Her monograph, *Hikāyat Abī l-Qāsim: A Literary Banquet* (Edinburgh University Press, 2016), and her translation, *Selections from the Art of Party-Crashing in Medieval Iraq*, both focus on the figure of the uninvited guest. She also edited a co-authored textbook titled *Baghdad at the Centre of a World: 8th-13th Century* (Theran Press, 2020). She is currently the PI of a Leverhulme-funded research project, 'A Sorcerer's Handbook', and she is the convener of the University of Exeter's Magic and Esotericism research group.

Anika Sprague (University College Roosevelt, 2021) is working towards her bachelor of arts degree with a focus on antiquity and philosophy, before pursuing a master's and PhD in maritime archaeology. Her research interests include ancient Greek myth, art, ritual, music, and herbal medicine, as well as the evolutionary history of shipbuilding, ancient maritime routes, hieroglyphic studies, and metaphysics. She is currently working as a SCUBA diving instructor teaching deep, mixed-gas, and shipwreck-penetration specialties.

Simone Stals (University College Roosevelt, 2021) has studied history, archaeology, ancient history, heritage and museum studies at UCR and through extracurricular courses. They recognise the romanticization of the past and the Western-instigated systems which support and perpetuate such understanding. They look forward to both a master's and finding work in this field. Their research interests lie with various research topics, such as how mythology and philosophy interact in an ancient context and how this can be researched by material evidence from key everyday events such as burial rituals.

Danise van Hal (BA, University College Roosevelt) has studied antiquity, art history, and rhetoric. Additionally, she developed an interest in musicology, which she further pursued by researching music of ancient Greece. She is currently continuing her studies in archaeology at the University of Groningen. Her study on the production of *auloi*, ancient Greek flutes, will soon appear in *The Value of Making* (Helle Hochscheid and Ben Russell eds., Brepols: in press 2021).

Daantje van de Linde (University College Roosevelt, 2021) is a liberal arts and science student with a specialisation in antiquity, rhetoric, and psychology. She holds a particular interest in both heritage management and development studies, with a specific focus on and curiosity toward African histories, cultures, and identities. Her latest research focuses on the colonial and postcolonial interpretations of the West-African archaeological record, located in modern-day Nigeria. In September 2021, she aims to continue her studies in the field of heritage and archaeology.

KEYNOTE BIOGRAPHY

Michael J. Strand is Professor of Art and Head of Visual Arts at North Dakota State University. With a background as a functional potter, Michael's work has moved seamlessly into social and community engagement while remaining dedicated to the traditional object as he investigates the potential of craft as a catalyst for social change.

In May 2016, Strand's 'Misfit Cup Liberation Project' took place at the Yingge Ceramics Museum in Taipei, Taiwan. This work is an extension of recent national and international projects that led to Strand being named '2015 Ceramic Artist of the Year" by *Ceramics Monthly*. He is a 2014-16 Bush Foundation Fellow who focused on the potential of functional design to facilitate cross-cultural communication extending from Brazil, Taiwan, South Africa, and Europe. Strand was also recently elected to the International Academy of Ceramics (IAC) – and joined the board of Trustees for the American Craft Council in 2016.

Strand's work has been published internationally, with articles in *American Craft*, *Ceramics Monthly*, *Studio Potter*, *Hemslojen*, *The Chronicle of Higher Education* and *Public Art Review*. His work is also included in Yale University Press publication '40 Under 40: Craft Futures' and the recently published Bloomsburg Press publication – 'Nation Building: Craft and Contemporary Culture', authored and edited by Smithsonian curator Nicholas Bell.

Strand lectures and leads workshops extensively including recent engagements at the Smithsonian American Art Museum in Washington D.C., Haystack Mountain School of Crafts, American Craft Council, Museum of Contemporary Craft in Portland, OR, University Federal San Joao Del Rei in Brazil, and Universidad Caxias Do Sul in Caxias Do Sul, Brazil.

INTRODUCTION

INTRODUCTION

Helle Hochscheid & Peter Schultz

Humanities/Survival

The initial agenda for this book and the colloquium upon which it is based was quite straightforward: We wanted to bring together an international group of interdisciplinary scholars and a group of students from a small University College in the Netherlands to ask questions about 'heritage' and its communication across a range of institutional platforms. The participants came from many different countries and backgrounds and held a wide range of world views and values. Among them were artists, activists, linguists, historians, poets, anthropologists, environmentalists, archaeologists, musicians, and psychologists – the list goes on. What all these people had in common was a love for the humanities, the arts, and our shared human heritage. In conceiving our program, some of the preliminary problems that we had in mind were: Who decides when, how, and where heritage is studied, published, and consumed? What is the role of ideology in heritage studies and heritage management? How should – or shouldn't – governments and NGOs shape our images of the past? What tactics do schools, parks, libraries, and museums deploy to engage both students of heritage and the general public? And, perhaps one of the most important sets of questions: How is 'heritage' *itself* defined, by whom, and why?

As we organized the colloquium, these seemed like significant issues; it seemed like an important project that framed important problems. And not just for us as professional academics in the humanities, but even more so for our students.

And then – less than six months after we met in Middelburg – the world changed.

In mere moments, in a scenario that still feels more like science fiction than reality, a global pandemic and our subsequent responses jolted and disrupted institutions and processes around the world. COVID-19 – the microscopic Godzilla that infectious disease experts had been warning us about for decades – had arrived on the scene. And it was ugly. Markets crashed, businesses folded, universities closed their doors. The virus was immediately politicized – in the ancient sense of that word – with varying degrees of success. In New Zealand and Thailand, for example, the monster was engaged via ruthless scientific competence and was contained with minimal economic damage and little loss of human life. In the United States, the beast was first ignored, then fed . . . and went on to kill over half a million citizens.

This new reality has allowed us – and has forced us – to ask an entirely new set of questions about our initial questions. For example: With a dangerous creature loose within the global *polis*, are questions about how heritage is consumed really 'important'? How do we begin to define what 'important' means within the context of a global pandemic which has wrought havoc upon our most vulnerable populations? Are the events of the last year yet further proof that we have an ever greater need for 'dragon-slaying' fields like STEM and a far less urgent need for 'decadent luxuries' like the humanities? Why should we care about defining heritage when more than 3.5 million people have died? And, perhaps one of the most important questions: If we don't dare to ask questions like these, right now, is there any real role for disciplines that concern themselves with cultural heritage in the first place?

These questions are not just metacritical. They rest at the foundation of our disciplines in both a pragmatic and a political sense. They are pragmatic questions because the pandemic has seen record layoffs and hiring freezes in the arts, heritage-related fields, and the humanities across the U.S. and Europe, a trend that threatens the basis of the liberal academy. They are political questions because in academic contexts, as well as in society in general, the arts and humanities – marginalized already – often have not been vocally championed by their own practitioners during this crisis for what they are: the foundation of our shared intellectual and cultural traditions. When we fight to save lives, do we just fight for raw, biological existence? Or do we fight for our relationships, our communities, our values – for the very idea of 'human heritage' itself?

Indeed, it is precisely at moments like these that the true value of the diverse and interconnected fields of heritage studies prove their undeniable worth. Yes, COVID-19 is an immediate biological threat, but it has also highlighted entrenched cultural and social problems that extend beyond science. What has C-19 revealed about inequalities in society and their attendant histories? What has the pandemic shown us about humanity's fractured political and social responses and those responses' cultural, political, and historical contexts? What can humans' past responses to similar situations teach us about the present one – and can we allow ourselves to be taught? What are the psychological and sociological challenges associated with extended isolation? How have the arts become tools for raw survival? Questions like these all point to issues that are far broader and more long-lasting than the immediate public health emergency now being brought under control. Thinking hard and critically about our global, social, and personal reactions to C-19 is every bit as crucial as pushing for new scientific data and findings.

Those deep processes of self-conscious and critical thought – the ability to think systematically and historically about human behavior, storytelling, and traditions – is precisely the skillset that we have always cultivated as teachers and students of the humanities and human heritage. It is through history, political science, art, archaeology, sociology, and psychology that we seek a deeper understanding of the entrenched mentalities and social dynamics that have framed humanity's response to this, or any other, crisis. By encouraging ourselves and our students to look deep within our own stories and traditions – and how these things interconnect – these linked disciplines prompt us to engage with this pandemic on levels deeper than biology, levels that are not simply interesting luxuries but, rather, profoundly important phenomena integral to our survival as human beings.

How does this work, in concrete terms?

First, *innovation*. The study of human heritage – the arts, the humanities, and their attendant traditions – is the study of human creativity and ingenuity, of human making and thinking. Revolution has always come from joining disparate, pre-existing concepts. Steve Jobs combined ideas from Chinese calligraphy with ideas from computer science to create the Apple aesthetic. There would be no submarines without Jules Verne. Your phone is based on plastic props from *Star Trek*. The design of a Tesla owes almost everything to Stanley Kubrick's *2001: A Space Odyssey* – itself a story about telling stories about the nature of technology and innovation and its triumphs and risks. 'What is now proved,' William Blake wrote, 'was once only imagined.' In order to innovate, we must make creative leaps. Students of cultural heritage are exceptionally equipped to do this because this is the core of their discipline. Indeed, the basis of a humanities education is the ostensible exposure to the breadth of human knowledge. Literature, history, philosophy, art, social sciences, archaeology – the entire basis of our shared heritage – is the basis of our future, by default and by definition. There can be no true innovation without the understanding of tradition. Do we – at great cost – reinvent the wheel in a panic with each new crisis?

Or do we realize that our tradition of innovation is one that spans all of our shared human history and that the efficiency of our responses relies on our grasp of the past?

Second, *storytelling*. While it's been all the rage on social media for folks to call themselves 'digital storytellers', this idea is as old as the cave paintings at Leang Tedongnge. Organizations, businesses, and governments all want employees who can communicate in a way that furthers their agendas and their missions. Fluency in the traditions of storytelling isn't a 'decadent luxury'. It's essential. Indeed, the last year has shown how profoundly important stories – both true and false – can influence the fundamental realities of our day-to-day lives and our survival as a species. Moreover, for organizations, governments, and corporations operating in multicultural societies, the unambiguous cross-cultural communication with customers, colleagues, and business partners is crucial for success. But this kind of communication is hard – especially if you focused all your studies on physics. Our shared human heritage is a bridge, one that is necessary for the true interconnection of all humans. This isn't all just window dressing, either. Research has shown that reading fiction and studying art increases your ability to empathize with others. Those Chinese, South American, Russian, French, English, and world literature courses you took? They made you better able to relate to people who are not like you. They taught you how to think against your gut feeling, to practice *dissoi logoi*, so you could find out where that other person is coming from. Think about it like this: If you had to pick, who would you rather have in the field opening a new market? A person who can calculate the demographics of the audience really fast or a genius communicator? People do business with people they like, those who can easily, and authentically, empathize with them. What is more, empathetic storytelling is the first step towards mutual help and support in communities. Telling stories well can bridge time, space, and people. Communities whose members can know each other, understand each other, and feel for each other are more stable, healthier, and more prosperous. In this way, the ability to communicate in both directions – conveying and receiving what is being offered – is one of the most essential skills that people can learn. Does it matter if you have a miracle vaccine if you can't convince people to take it?

Third, *synthesis and analysis*. Structural assessment and pattern recognition is central to studying human heritage. Whether learning a Medieval philosopher's ethical system, the aims of an ancient Greek sculptor, or the economic theories of Tudor England, students engaged in the study of our shared history consume vast amounts of information, make sense of it, and then synthesize, formulate, and critique what they've learned against the background of our shared human experience. Is this always comprehensive? Of course not. It's not supposed to be. It's supposed to spark and foster a set of skills that thrives on ambiguity, comparison, and juxtaposition. Students who study human heritage can understand complex practical and theoretical arguments, discern their strengths and weaknesses, and formulate responses. The business of the humanities is the practical analysis and synthesis of complex data and the use of the same to craft lines of discussion that make sense of things. We didn't just need scientists telling us what was happening at the beginning of C-19 – we needed historians! Whether the raw data are examples of symbolism in *Portrait of the Artist as a Young Man*, or the patterns on Peruvian pottery, or consumer behaviour for a potential new shop, the skills are the same: finding meaning in the data, and convincing others that your interpretation is viable and important. This works in the seminar room and in the board room, and often in the field, too. Studying the humanities inculcates an open mind and a penchant for asking questions. And when the answers are found, asking some more about those. These are invaluable tools when confronting conformist thinking, the critical evaluation of new ideas, or a global disaster. All the numbers in the world don't mean anything if they can't be put into contexts that make sense.

Lastly, *appreciating the big picture.* Life is more than what we can see in a test tube. Great leaders respect the micro-view – but they can also see and communicate the big picture. They can see where a country or an organization is headed, and they can see what it needs to do to get there. Curiosity, humility, and the understanding that there is way more to the world than a single point of view – these are all qualities that separate great leaders from the throng. And C-19 has provided some important opportunities to assess these necessary qualities in the world's leaders – qualities that are not quantifiable but, rather, very much about quality. Moreover, asking the right questions about the world means having a general awareness of the history of these questions across time and space. Indeed, how do you begin to know what questions to ask without the rigorous study of past answers? Studying the humanities trains us to ask and attempt to answer the big questions about society, politics, art, and life. Professors in heritage studies, or in fact in humanities at large, help train our students to figure out why the pieces appear as they do, how they relate, how they don't, and how they fit together. We teach people to debate how things *should* be, how to *dream*. When faced with a global challenge, do we want leaders locked in their own minds? Or human beings versed in the tragedies and triumphs of our shared human tradition?

Art, literature, philosophy, history, and archaeology are the arenas in which societies debate who they are and what they want to be. It is impossible to read great works of literature, to read great history, to delve into the history of philosophy or of craft, and not ponder the timeless human questions. When we read Thucydides, we're reading our own shared history and values. When we study ancient architecture in Africa, we're looking into our own human past and the basic principles shared by all peoples. When we think about how a Native American community communicates its ethos to the next generation, we are engaged in a profound study of timeless human morals. Students of our shared heritage wrestle with and engage ethical issues – and they know what these issues are when they see them. Those of us who study human heritage don't have a nice, neat curve of progress against which we measure our development. Instead, we are the caretakers of something even more profound, something truly universal: the messy, glorious, beautiful struggle of our plight to find and create *meaning* for ourselves, meaning that is truthful and just. In such meaning lies the relevance of our existence. These things not only give us joy, they are the foundations of – and the reasons for – our survival.

Teaching/Research

Speaking the Past was a colloquium comprised of university students and international scholars, held at University College Roosevelt, a Liberal Arts and Sciences college in Middelburg, the Netherlands. The students who participated had innocently enrolled for a course on heritage called 'The Global Artefact' – taught by Helle Hochscheid – before being thrown into what they perceived as a James Bond-style shark tank, engaging with and responding to *real* researchers, scholars even, and presenting their work at this forum. Universities tend to separate research from teaching. Teaching is often seen as a burden that one has to take on so as to be allowed research time. In designing our colloquium, some chemical reaction happened, and we broke through that research-teaching barrier.

The original idea was that if our students are to become successful individuals in society – successful in the sense of being able and motivated to apply and convey their capacity for innovation, storytelling, and critical analysis – we needed to open the door to the rather colder world out there during their time in university.

Presenting to your class can be terrifying to some, but presenting to 'real' scholars is as daunting as climbing Mt. Etna in full pyroclastic eruption. *What if they think I'm talking rubbish? How can I say something that is worthwhile in such a context, having done only some undergrad studying? What if they laugh at me?* You can say a hundred times that nobody would do that, but the fear of not believing oneself good enough will paralyze most students. Which is exactly why it is so much better to conquer those worries as an undergraduate. Because the things we hope to teach, as important as they are, are irrelevant if we cannot boost confidence and conviction 'in application', too. It takes a lot of guts to stand up in front of an audience and voice your views, arguments, and feelings about an issue, even if they contradict those of others in the room.

Confidence was a key ingredient, but it had to be balanced by respect for the researchers and artists and for their work. This balance was built into the assignment given to both groups: Researchers sent students articles on a heritage topic in their respective fields of expertise. Students could indicate preference for these articles individually or in pairs, and wrote a response to the article that was assigned to them. Most students got in touch with 'their' scholar to exchange ideas. Some disagreed with them. Some reacted to the topic and took it in new directions. Some confirmed the notions in their article by coming at it from a different direction. The scope and variety of the responses surprised and impressed us infinitely. And while nerves ran high, the communication that had been established between researchers and undergrad researchers took the sting out of it. By lunch break, creativity was bubbling, scholarship was shifting, and people were genuinely moved.

In terms of innovation, storytelling, and critical analysis, the day was fruitful beyond anything we could have anticipated. Despite the differences between the participants – in age, background, academic status, worldview, and so on – the world felt whole.

That achievement is partly the result of the setup, but mostly it is the result of what every participant delivered and the shared dynamic that this produced. For this, we are deeply grateful. And it is why the fruit of this work of heritage, this fundamental discourse of our human condition, is here before you: for its beauty to linger and its message endure.

Acknowledgements

The October 2019 colloquium in Middelburg and the publication of this book would not have been possible without the generous help from University College Roosevelt's Undergraduate Research Fund. Many thanks to the dean of UCR, Bert van den Brink, for his opening words on the day, and his support for this endeavor. Thanks also to Albert Clement, the head of the Arts & Humanities Department at UCR, for his assistance, especially with the pre-conference workshop at the culture house Kuijperspoort in Middelburg. Sylvia Radius kindly hosted us at this location, and Sophie Krier, our then-resident artist and art and design instructor, brought her students and expertise to the conference and helped organize the pre-conference workshop – to both our warmest thanks. We are truly grateful to The Rourke Art Gallery + Museum and to Theran Press for their generous support of this project and its publication.

We are deeply indebted to the Research Institute for American Studies in Middelburg, in particular to Giles Scott Smith, Dario Fazzi, Damian Pargas, and Cees Heere who were kind enough to host the keynote lecture and reception. Special thanks are also owed Michael Strand, Professor of Art and Head of Visual Arts at North Dakota State University, who waived his fees, gave an amazing pre-conference workshop, and delivered an awesome keynote lecture. Finally, we would like to thank the participants in the colloquium who spent their time and energy making this the miraculous day that it was.

THE PROCEEDINGS

Make Pepsi Pay:
Surviving With Integrity under the Corporate University

Mike Lippman

Unfortunately, in the academy's Brave New World, survival depends on entrepreneurial thinking. This is not necessarily good, but I fear we no longer have any real options. Struggling against this destiny, while potentially noble, seems futile, even tragically doomed. I first realized this, ironically, while teaching a 500-person megacourse on Oedipus and Electra myths at the University of Arizona. UA had already embraced a model called 'Responsibility Centered Management' (RCM): a system that essentially turns every unit on campus into its own mini business (more on that later). My current employer, University of Nebraska, Lincoln, just announced their own upcoming transformation to this RCM model. After years of my insisting on its inevitability, I transformed from Cassandra into Sarah Connor. Now that the Terminators have arrived, at least I'm well trained to stay alive.

Back to my UA Oedipus class. I realized that my academic survival, given my non-traditional scholarly persona, depended on my doing exactly what my father had wanted years ago: to take the path I had so forcibly rejected. In my early 20s, my father, owner of a NJ car-rental/leasing business (all the stereotypes that just popped into mind are probably true), tried to convince me to join the 'family business'. Like Darth Vader in *Empire*: 'Together we can rule the NJ car rental business as father and son . . .' Luke-like, I shouted: 'No! I'll never join you . . . never!' And thus I hurled myself in the grad-school abyss. Twenty years later, in the Oedipus course, I had an Aristotelian *anagnorisis*. Owning the skill-set for a successful car dealer who could take on the corporations and thrive in NJ is the only reason why I'm still academically afloat. That's what I'm here to talk about.

Fast foward. I'm now at UNL being told that digital humanities were the future. Teaching, recruiting majors, making Homerathons and all that exciting shit wasn't enough. Join the digital revolution! Fortunately, since I had long been on the editorial board of *Didaskalia*, the international online journal for ancient drama and reception, I knew that Amy Cohen, the editor-in-chief, was stepping down (her funding sadly cut).[1] A few emails later, others invited me to throw my hat into the ring, in part because they trusted I could find a way to fund it.

That, of course, was the trick. After all, *Didaskalia* remains committed to being an open-access journal. So, I had to fund it in some manner that didn't involve selling out principles or being held hostage to the agenda of some external financial source. At the outset, my department seemed eager to participate. In UNL's College of Arts and Sciences, Classics is the only department without a graduate program. As an R1 institution recently added to the Big Ten, we are thus pressured to compete with, say, the University of Michigan. So, an international journal would heighten our prestige. Thus, for the first few years, the department guaranteed funding from our own pool of donor money. I, however, was instructed to discover other sources, pronto, on the assumption that the department's resources were ultimately limited.

The best way to accomplish this would be to convince another office on campus, at the dean's level or above, to bear the expense. I wanted to ensure that the journal would not only remain a regular provider of content: articles, reviews, and the like, but also that *it itself* become an undergraduate research project. That way it could offer both genuine research opportunities for Classics undergrads, but also – and this is very important now to upper adminstration – teach them 'real world skills'.

---

[1] www.didaskalia.net.

My original plan was to update a part of the site first designed for teachers: a pedagogical sidebar/aid, with constantly updated bibliography, slides, links, etc. In order to raise some funds, I thought I could assign an archival project, such as: 'All the ancient drama produced in Nebraska'. This might bring grants, funding from which could then be partly diverted to the journal's overhead costs. When I brought my ideas to the *Didaskalia* board, however, a better idea just fell into my lap.

Fiona MacIntosh, director of the Archive for the Producion of Greek and Roman Drama, thought my archival research ideas were redundant, given her own work. But, she had a minor problem and thought I could help. She had received grants to transform her excellent book, *Medea in Performance 1500-2000*, into a free, web-accessible 'e-book'. I had to learn what an e-book was. In the *APGRD* model, it is like a book comprised of screen displays you see in modern museums. There's a minimal amount of text, but you can press sections to interact further: Hear so-and-so reciting famous lines; hear background music; expand a city map, photos, videos, etc., etc. To get an idea of a finished product, visit either the *Didaskalia* website or the *APGRD* website and follow the appropriate links.[2]

In any event, Fiona had turned her one book on *Medea* into an e-book and was developing a second based on her book on *Agamemnon*. As a condition for her grants, she had promised to train other schools to join the long-term project. She then proposed a partnership with my students and *Didaskalia*. The Oxford team would provide training sessions with my undergraduates via Skype throughout the year to show them the nuts and bolts of production as well as discuss successes and failures from the first

---

[2] Didaskalia link above (and if you use that one, it helps the journal!). However, the *APGRD*, our partners, deserve 'hits' too and it is a spectacular resource. Explore both! http://www.apgrd.ox.ac.uk/.

two e-books. Then, my *Didaskalia* team would construct the third book. (Now underway: the reception history of the *Antigone*.) Then, theoretically, we could trade back and forth and cover the rest of ancient theater forever. After hammering out details that summer, the Oxford team led eight different training sessions during the fall of 2018. Then I – with the help of my colleague Matthew Loar – worked with the students to get a headstart on the *Antigone* book. In summer 2019, I led five students on the team to Oxford for a few weeks to consult the archive and collect raw material to build what will emerge as the completed e-book.

The e-book project was thus linked with *Didaskalia* literally and figuratively. We put links on our site to the *Medea* e-book and committed to linking the site to all future e-books in the series. In return, *APGRD* linked to *Didaskalia* and made public announcements about their selection of UNL, as if selected from a competitive field, as the perfect academic partner. Everyone now looks good on every angle, everyone increases online traffic; and thus, we have a propaganda win-win. My university is thrilled because of this high-profile undergraduate collaboration with Oxford – a partnership they can display to alumni donors. Thus the journal could remain a priority while we do high-level undergraduate research that would otherwise be difficult to accomplish. Simultaneously, undergraduates learn numerous hard skills on the e-book programs, web design, high-level research, and project management. They're working as a team, traveling abroad, writing professional emails, as well as reducing complex chunks of information to easily readable formats for our prospective audience. From the point of view of job training, the project is spectacular.

Where did the money come from, though, for this large student work force, you might quite reasonably ask. One option might have been to create a course and give them credit for the experience. This, however, would mean that just anyone could enroll and I might be stuck with some deadweight students who would drag down the high level of the project's quality. Instead, I stumbled upon another income source which has completely altered my approach to all my outside projects (including the Homerathon).[3] Basically, I found a corporate sponsor without selling out. Let me explain.

Each major campus in the US (and, I expect, most smaller ones) must make regular business decisions: Coke or Pepsi? Apple or PC? Bookstores, coffee shops, franchises in the student union, office supplies: all are done via large scale contracts so that the campus (or if you're at a state school, the entire state system) makes an exclusive choice to hold the students essentially hostage to one brand while on campus. One of the things I learned at UA is that many of these large-scale business transactions come with a bonus: a sort of bribe/conscience payoff. (You see my NJ showing.) Basically, a bundle of cash is a public kickback to the campus to ensure brand loyalty. The 'payoff', which for all I know *also* includes stereotypical illegal envelopes of money, often manifests in a legal way as bonus student programming. At UA, I found a fund sponsored by Xerox to encourage professors to engage with students outside of class, like taking them to see a play. I barely had to fill out a form to get the money. I was never denied, and the fund seemed limitless. At some point (funny side story) because I drew on this tap more than most in the humanities, someone once offered me a credit card to use whenever I wanted. Moral person that I am, I refused, knowing that I'd have bankrupted the state of Arizona with such power. I'd have held study sessions for 500

---

[3] For the Homerathon pivot under COVID-19, see homerathon.com. For earlier Homerathons, a Google search will show you many, but for 2019, see: https://mediahub.unl.edu/media/11902. For my earlier iteration in Arizona, see: https://www.insidehighered.com/news/2011/05/12/long-reads, with the link to a video therein.

students at the finest restaurants in the city every night of the week.

In any event, at UNL, some money comes from the fairly wealthy Pepsico. No Coke products are allowed on campus. I learned this after being scolded once after a nighttime film screening. I had provided pizza, but everything else was 'pot-luck'. Some students brought cookies and so forth, but one student brought a case of Dr. Pepper. Those cans in the trash put me deep in the dog house. I was formally interrogated by the Pepsi Secret Police (meaning some administrator called me and told me how inappropriate this all was). Clearly the garbage man ratted me out. He's dead now. No, just kidding.

At UNL there is something called a UCARE grant for students, funded by Pepsi. This money goes to students involved in large-scale research projects and provides about $2,500 per semester. It pays for ten hours of work per week for the two 15-week periods and then there's another UCARE for the summer. Each professor is eligible to supervise up to three students. My situation drastically changed when I discovered I could flexibly interpret this word 'research' on UCARE terms. At first, it was unlikely that an undergrad could join me on my own *real* research projects, just because of the level of Greek and background knowledge they'd need to be helpful. Thus, I had not seriously considered this financial source. Supervising a student's research project – like an honors thesis or capstone – is not only time-consuming for me (and uncompensated), but requires a very self-motivated student pool. But, I learned how loosely one can interpret 'research'. A kind of internship, whether it be for *Didaskalia*, the newly acquired e-book project, or running the Homerathon – all count as 'undergraduate research', eligible for UCARE dollars. And, because all three projects could be spun not only as typical humanities research (which require justifications for applicability to Pepsi and the outside world), these projects all required more broadly applicable 'job building skills': running a large operation, learning publication and editing programs, advertising, running social media, and so forth. Once I convinced the head of UCARE how I'd be running things, she was so enthused that I was given special permission to go outside the normal application process just to expedite my idea. I now just essentially pick the best-suited students. I learned that the humanities had been woefully underrepresented for UCARE, partly because the average professor's research didn't have room for undergraduates, and if they did, the work offered was generally tedious and lonely data entry. Thus, the undergraduates *preferred* more social jobs at Starbucks. Whereas the sciences – which did use UCARE students – also had plenty of graduate students, so the undergraduate opportunities, such as they existed, offered far less in the way of opportunity. But if the students could get them, their projects were easier to translate into careers. My undergraduates, however, were placed in leadership positions. This made the people running the program, the administration, and I have heard, Pepsico, all very happy.

So happy, in fact, that I've been getting more exceptions left and right. The original limit, as I mentioned, is three students per professor. Last year, Matthew Loar joined me on the e-book project, so his three students joined mine. Because my three had other responsibilities as well, he was able to make his into part-time workers on the e-book (4-5 hours per week) and part-time graders/TAs for his large-lecture myth class (thus saving our department several thousand dollars). A third professor took on two more UCARE students, largely an approved illusion. She just signed their paperwork, while they joined my already existing team (see how Sopranos-esque this all is?). So last year I had, in essence, eight students, all paid to work 5-10 hours per week, committed to building this e-book, editing *Didaskalia*, and creating and implementing the Homerathon.

Last year's plan was so successful, I was given special permission this year for more exceptions. If you are not familiar, UNL had a large controversy with Turning Point and there were repercussions with the state house and possible funding cuts.[4] Let us just say that last year at UNL, the humanities were not quite popular. Thus, having my students (five of whom are women) visit the end-of-the-semester display of posters at the state house made a good impression at a critical time. And so administrators gaze down more favorably. When Matthew Loar left UNL, I was given permission to add his UCARE students to my own, giving me five for summer 2019 (thus the fully paid Oxford trip) and six for 2019-20. I also agreed to be part of an experimental program (same funding source) called FYRE (another unknown acronym), whereby freshmen are given a research job. They spend half the time and get half the pay, but they also get a community and some work-study substitute to keep them both involved – and, more importantly to the admins – retained. So now I still have a team of eight (two freshman 'interns', five former students from the previous year, and one new student) working for me. My new concept is to overlap all three projects even more, as if it were a business with team leaders, where everyone can be moved around weekly as needed. I met with the vice-chancellor (the UCARE person's boss's boss) to see if I could continue breaking the rules next year and retain my exception of six to eight people moving forward. Because I am running technically three different projects combined as one, she has given her enthusiastic support and I am now essentially exempt from the normal procedures.

Thus, I have a staff of six to eight students with about 60-70 weekly hours of labor, funded by Pepsi, for running a publication, writing a book that helps fund that publication, and putting on our annual Homerathon. Additionally, part of their job is to fundraise so our capital can rise even more.

[4] See https://www.aaup.org/report/academic-freedom-and-tenure-university-nebraska-lincoln.

They write grants, find internal sources of revenue within the university, and so forth. Furthermore, the raised profile of all these projects in terms of university (and larger) press has made the admins and donors all the more eager to support them/send us money, since I've made it quite clear that the situation is: no *Didaskalia*, no e-book. I've learned a great deal about how to spin the projects and make the school feel like they're getting more than they've put in and it seems to be working. I've been given two course reductions to keep running my 'business' – to keep creating these 'products'. I have also just been asked to take on a part-time appointment at the Entrepeneurial School, a request that completely – and pleasantly – shocked me when it came through, but something I am sure would have greatly pleased my father.

I'm not quite sure what this all means, but one thing is for sure: running Classics like a business, and thinking in business terms does not mean that we need to compromise our 'product' – nor must we somehow be less involved in Classics than we were. I think we can remain Classicists, pumping out teaching and research and other creative projects, in such a way that it will be productive, and profitable. I do think, however, we really need to reconsider our model and approach, and not feel like the business mindset – which is, unfortunately, not going anywhere – must involve a futile, tragic struggle.

Thank you.[5]

---

[5] I want to thank Peter Schultz, Helle Hochscheid, Cady Rutter, and absolutely every participant in *Speaking the Past* for their feedback, friendship, and just the spectacular experience from start to finish. I want to especially thank Danise van Hal for her exceptional and – I say with pride, humility, and rueful self-awareness – more professional response to my informal paper.

Think Business, Study Arts & Humanities:
A Response to Mike Lippman

Danise van Hal

When I first read Mike Lippman's paper, it struck me as odd that it said scholars are not trained to be business people as opposed to probably engineers or scientists. To be honest, I simply thought the statement was not true. While I had not looked into the issue beforehand, I did remember being told about entrepreneurs at universities countless times before. Perhaps this was due to where I grew up – in Twente. Since my secondary school was only a half-hour train ride away from the University of Twente (UT), in the East of the Netherlands, my secondary encouraged us to go to several of their open days. As is customary on such days, universities tell stories of their achievements, which included the number of new start-ups for the UT. They claim to have reached over 1,000 spin-offs by now; on average, fifty new businesses are created every year. This includes quite well-known brands, such as: Booking.com, Demcon, and Thuisbezorgd.nl – a student favourite at our university.[1]

To sustain such initiatives in the region, Novel-T offers support which is not exclusive to the UT; students of Saxion, the local University of Applied Sciences, can also profit. This is why I believed the statement we started with to be false. When I read the description by Novel-T more carefully, however, I started to see where this claim had come from. It states that 'Twente is one of the top three technology regions in the Netherlands and is known for its entrepreneurial character'.[2] Of course, I knew

---

[1] 'Support for startups | Business & Innovation', Universiteit Twente, accessed October 20, 2019, https://www.utwente.nl/en/business/support-for-start-ups/.
[2] 'Focus areas', Novel-T., accessed October 20, 2019, https://novelt.com/en/focus-areas/.

that the UT was technology-focused; this was why I decided to study somewhere further away from home. What I did not base this choice on, was the emphasis of the entrepreneurial mindset. Moreover, Novel-T states that they support the technical UT and Saxion – both of which are clearly technical. This is also reflected in Novel-T's aim to 'come up with smart *technology-driven* solutions for future issues'.[3]

I still had some hope left for the scholars among us; perhaps this was not a non-technical view. To check this, I turned to secondary literature. In an article on entrepreneurial intention, findings show that university type and study major can play a considerable role. This was an interesting statement after the introduction, in which entrepreneurial intention was highly praised in economic development. Entrepreneurship was said to contribute to inventions, efficiency, and even job creation. While this is beneficial to the technical field, it seems equally valuable for other (academic) fields, including those of arts and humanities. Yet, the results showed that entrepreneurial intention was higher in students from technological universities compared to those who attended other types. Moreover, technological universities indeed focused more on entrepreneurship in education. As a result, entrepreneurial intent was increased.[4]

This was confirmed by other research on study majors and entrepreneurship, specifically focused on education in humanities and social sciences. Unsurprisingly, business sciences scored highest in all categories – business knowledge, skills, and attitudes. The humanities students in their research scored the lowest in skills and knowledge regarding entrepreneurship. Furthermore, they scored second-lowest in the attitude category. The most striking difference was found in business knowledge in which humanities students scored less than half of the business science students

<hr>

[3] 'Focus areas', Novel-T.
[4] Zhang, Duysters, and Cloodt, 'Role of Entrepeneurship Education', 623-41.

– 2.29 versus 5.05. While gaps in the other two categories were less shocking, differences are still very noticeable.[5] It was at this point that I had to agree with the statement; scholars are indeed not trained business people. Rather than simply accepting this, however, I started wondering *why* academics are not trained to have entrepreneurial knowledge, intention, and everything else needed for a business mindset.

Frankly, I felt a bit left out as an arts and humanities student. After reading about the positive consequences of entrepreneurial mindsets over and over again, I wanted to be included. If the only way for me to gain access to this mindset would be to attend a business or technological university, I believe this to be unfair. I decided to give looking for entrepreneurial support one more try. After all, I had only looked for support systems on the website of a technological university. Perhaps, I just had not found or heard of a system before because I had not searched well enough. Since I study at quite a small university – University College Roosevelt in Middelburg – I decided to first look at Utrecht University (UU), of which UCR is part.

I was happily surprised when I found three support systems. Utrecht Holdings offers students help with commercial advice on patentable inventions. Utrecht Center for Entrepreneurship offers courses and events to sustain their business mindset. UtrechtInc. offers advice on how to set up and maintain spin-off businesses. I thought I had hit the jackpot; since UU is not solely technologically or business-focused, they must be more inclusive. Students from other bachelor or master's studies must also have access to these systems set in place to foster entrepreneurship at UU. Unfortunately, UtrechtInc. turned out to be an undertaking of Utrecht University of Applied

[5] José Luis Vázquez-Burgete et al., 'Entrepeneurship Education', 33.

Sciences, a technical university in Utrecht, and UMC Utrecht – the medical department.[6] Again, humanities and social science studies appeared to be overlooked in the world of entrepreneurship.

I started to think that there was really no entrepreneurial hope for my major but did not want not to give up before combing through UCR's website. While we are small, we are also a liberal arts and sciences college. In practice, this means that we are allowed to choose our courses, building our personal curriculum. This is the reason why I am able to follow courses in antiquity, art history, and rhetoric all in the same bachelor study. As one can imagine, this can lead to much interconnectivity between different tracks. On our website, this is illustrated as listening to classical music while preparing for a thermodynamics course.[7] If this combination is possible, surely the entrepreneurship mindset should also be able to spread into the arts & humanities and social science department.

Connections to the province of Zeeland and Utrecht University are emphasised on the website. Thus, the groundwork already exists. All we would have to do as a university would be to allow the business mindset to be present in all four departments – not just in engineering and sciences but also arts & humanities and social sciences. At the very least, we could attempt to set up an inclusive support system which offers business advice and support for anyone interested, regardless of their major or department.

In response to this statement, a question was asked about how Middelburg could be more involved in UCR projects. While I have heard of certain projects such as internships at the Zeeuws Museum in art history class, I do not believe this to be the standard approach.

---

[6] 'Entrepeneurship', Utrecht University, accessed October 20, 2019, https://www.uu.nl/en/research/collaboration/entrepeneurship.
[7] 'Our Vision', University College Roosevelt, accessed October 20, 2019, https://www.ucr.nl/abou-ucr/discover/our-vision/.

Being able to work with local organisations or institutes outside of UCR is often still considered to be a special opportunity. Perhaps, projects would be undertaken more regularly or on a bigger scale if the business mindset would become more prominent at our university. Involving students in these business projects could help us prepare for the future, in which this knowledge is claimed to be important. After all, we need to make money to sustain ourselves; a business mindset could thus prove to be very useful.

By sending students out into the community, we can learn how to pitch ideas, request companies' help, and build a network. While it is possible to learn these skills after obtaining your bachelor or master's degree, it might be more difficult to obtain critical feedback on how well you performed these tasks. In a safe learning environment, mistakes can be made, can be learnt from, and can be improved upon. By offering students opportunities to start working on these business skills early on in life, universities can contribute to preparing their students for the real world.

Lastly, it was remarked that certain tracks such as the arts and design practice track do contain an entrepreneurial approach. The small businesses in the province of Zeeland are regularly included in the course material, which shows that there are opportunities. If the province of Zeeland has been open to working with students before, chances are that they would like to do so again. Therefore, let us embrace the example set by this track in the arts & humanities department and reach out in other tracks too. Let us all work towards a future in which everyone can reap the benefits of having a business mindset – regardless of study major or university type.

References

Vázquez-Burgete, J., A. Lanero, A. Raisiene, and M. García. 'Entrepreneurship Education in Humanities and Social Sciences: Are Students Qualified to Start a Business?'. *Verslas: Teorija ir Praktika* 13, no. 1 (2012): 27-35.

Zhang, Y., G. Duysters, and M. Cloodt. 'The Role of Entrepreneurship Education as a Predictor of University Students' Entrepreneurial Intention'. *International Entrepreneurship and Management Journal* 10, no. 3 (2013): 623-641.

Of Paper and Pixels: Reading in Flux

Michael Burke

Introduction

How will we be reading one hundred years from now, and why? This is the question that this paper seeks to explore. It is pertinent to reflect on this now, because today, anno 2020, we are in a liminal reading condition, positioned between paper and pixels; half digital, half analogue; half books, half screens. This is the situation today, but in order to fully understand where reading is now, and where it is plausibly going in the coming years, we first need to reflect on where it has come from.

The Reading Past

So how did we start reading, and when, and where, and how, and why? It is almost certain that reading evolved for human economic reasons in the ancient Sumerian civilization in Mesopotamia some 5,000 years ago. At the marketplaces, people would sell things to each other. Sometimes swaps would take place or people would owe each other and would compensate each other at a later date. This all had to be memorized, that is, until someone came up with the bright idea of making small markings in clay tablets. Then when the clay hardened it would remind that person of what they had exchanged with whom and who owed them, and voilà, as if by magic, you have the birth of writing and, by default, reading. At its essence, writing and reading are simply a means of what scholars in the sciences and social sciences today would term 'cognitive offload', through the processes of coding and decoding. Admittedly, this is not a very intellectual or romantic beginning for what would go on to become arguably one of the most cerebral and idealistic activities a human being could engage in.

These simple marks on clay gradually evolved from basic hieroglyph forms to a style of writing called cuneiform, which consisted of small triangular, wedge-shaped marks (from the Latin *cuneus*, 'wedge'). A further evolution took writing into the domain of ideograms, where symbols are used to represent ideas. This is where English and other languages are today. Of course, writing has evolved differently in other parts of the world, not least in China and Japan, where the characters that are used are essentially logograms.

Over thousands of years, across many ancient civilizations, humans moved from writing on clay tablets and carving in stone to writing on papyrus and later on velum/parchment. Reading evolved too, as originally it was only done aloud. Yes, those great ancient libraries in places like Alexandra and Pergamum would have had no 'quiet please' or 'silence' signs, like you might find in some of the world's leading academic libraries of today, like the Bodleian in Oxford. Rather, they would have been cacophonies of hullabaloo and noise, as scholars read aloud from scrolls. Silent reading, something we take for granted today, only became dominant in the later Roman period when accountants and civil servants found that they could audit and process texts much more quickly if they read silently, rather than aloud. Traces of our reading aloud heritage can still be seen today in the reading of religious texts in faiths such as Judaism and Islam.

In time, reading from scrolls of papyrus, and later velum, also changed ever more to the medium of bound books. Many Western books were of an early Christian nature, written and illuminated by monks in monasteries. These books were all hardbacks and ranged from the enormous and heavy to the tiny and light. They were often only found in private collections: in churches, monasteries, universities, and in the private houses of wealthy individuals. The invention of the printing press by Gutenberg in 1440 marks the start of a shift in book production and indeed book culture from the human to the mechanical and from objects possessed by the few, to objects possessed by the 'many'. Well, 'many' is perhaps an exaggeration given the low levels of literacy at the time, but certainly many more than heretofore had been the case. A good example of this is the 17th century diarist, Samuel Pepys. Pepys was not poor, rather, he was upper-middle class. He was an administrator for the English navy, based in London, and later a Member of Parliament. In his journal, he writes of the books he sought, purchased, read, and added to his library at home. When he died, he bequeathed his entire collection to his former college, Magdalene, at Cambridge, and since 1724 his books have been on display in a purpose-built room.

This process of printing, collecting, and distributing books to include an ever-expanding circle of readers in Western society sped up during the European Enlightenment period. It perhaps found its zenith after the advent of the paperback novel (also known as the softback/softcover) in the late 19th century. The paperback, so central to our reading habits today, was a mere chance discovery. Someone hit on the bright idea of selling cheaper, lighter books at railway stations so that commuters might have something to read during their journeys. In the age of Pepys in the 17th century, and right up to the 19th century, you had something called the 'penny dreadfuls' (Pepys collected them), but these were just cheap pamphlets/booklets in the beginning, not paperbacks: they were almost always short stories of dubious repute, as the name suggests. Today in 2020, it can be said that the paperback still reigns supreme in the analogue division of books, but it now has a peer (or is it a challenger?): the digital e-book.

The Reading Present

The impending 'death of the paper book' was first muted in the late 1990s with the mass advent of digital technologies. But it didn't die.

Things did indeed look grim around 2007 when Amazon launched its Kindle e-reader and digital sales were starting to outstrip paper sales but it somehow clung on and is even showing signs of recovery. Bookshops, and especially independent bookshops, have reported increased sales in the past three years.[1] Ironically, it is the e-reader that appears to be in rapid decline, despite its excellent e-ink technology. This invention limits eye fatigue and has the same impact on the human eye as a regular paper book does. This e-ink invention is in stark contrast to the ubiquitous LCD screens that are found on desktops, laptops, tablets, and mobile phones. Such screens have a much greater impact on the eye, causing fatigue and strain.[2] Upon reflection, it can be said that when the e-reader came out, it only seemed to appeal to a narrow group of middle-aged educated people. Young people and students largely eschewed it in favour of their other digital devices. It is fair to say that the only time most students consider borrowing their parent's e-reader, or purchasing one themselves, is if they are going on their summer vacation or taking a gap year. After all, who would want to carry a backpack full of heavy books when you can cram a borrowed e-reader full of cheap title downloads before you leave home?

If digital reading has found a new hardware home, then it is plausibly on the mobile phone. This poses a much greater threat to books than the e-reader did. About five years ago, *The Washington Post* and *New York Times* were reporting that young urban professionals appeared to be reading novels and some non-fiction books across devices.[3] In this scenario, a person might start reading a novel in book format at the breakfast table at home, hop on the subway to work, and continue reading the same novel on their mobile phone until

---

[1] Alison Flood, 'People are so happy we exist: Indie bookshops grow despite retail slump', *The Guardian*, January 10, 2020.
[2] See Benedetto et al., 2013; Jeong, 2012; and Siegenthaler et al., 2012.
[3] A. Alter, 'The Plot Twist: E-Book Sales Slip, and Print Is Far From Dead', *The New York Times*, September 22, 2015; and J. Maloney, 'The rise of phone reading', *The Wall Street Journal*, August 14, 2015.

they reached work. These reading habits would then be repeated on the way home. The question is, is this toggling across devices mainstream and if so, is it here to stay? Or is it maybe even a sign that we are on our way to switching to digital? A study conducted shortly afterwards suggested that this behaviour was not being reproduced by students on campuses, who were appearing to remain loyal to paper and books.[4]

Students were also largely shunning reading on mobile devices, despite screens having become larger in the past few years in order to facilitate more conducive interactions across various digital viewing activities. Indeed, there are even emerging technologies that include bendable/foldable devices. Of course, the primary drive behind this technology is not to create a better paperback novel reading experience, but rather to prevent screens from shattering when they are dropped. A further extension of this technology is the Samsung Galaxy Fold, a smart phone launched in the summer of 2019 that becomes a tablet when unfolded. When launched it was predictably beset with design faults, especially pertaining to the hinge and the thickness of the glass, but it was quickly superseded in February 2020 by the Samsung Galaxy Z Flip, with ultra-thin folding glass and a hideaway hinge. When folded, it is much smaller than regular smartphones and easily fits into a user's pocket. Indeed, many of the tactile reasons avid readers give for not wanting to switch from analogue to digital reading is that they are too accustomed to bending and folding their paperbacks while reading curled up on their bed or in their favourite armchair. Advancing technology in bendable screens on mobile devices is arguably well on its way to making this objection obsolete.

Such haptic and ergonomic reasons are often given in qualitative feedback as to why readers of literary novels still shun the device

---

[4] See Burke and Bon, 'Locations and Means', 205-232.

in favour of the book.[5] Another is a locative reason: When people read in the park or at the beach or just at home lying in their beds at night before sleeping, they appear to prefer to do so with a 'natural' product (paper), as opposed to a synthetic one (plastic and glass). Olfactory reasons also play a role in this choice, namely, many readers tend to delight in the smell of books. This can be new books (the smell of print and ink, which is often toxic) or old books, that almond aroma which, if the truth be told, is just rotting paper and decomposing glue, often made from the bones of farm animals and horses' hooves. Typically, the market provides for the needs of the consumer and for those readers who use e-readers still; they can buy sprays/aerosols which can be applied to the plastic and glass of digital devices that will make them smell like old books.

Mark Twain once wrote that news of his death had been greatly exaggerated, and so it is with the reported death of the book. Books are proving to be remarkably resilient. We are, it seems, in a period of reading flux between paper and pixels. Having said this, though, we must realize that we are still only at the very beginning of the digital revolution in reading. It is not the end. It is not even the beginning of the end. In fact, it is not even the end of the beginning; it's just 'the beginning'. In spite of its current good health, sustained by the readers of present, like you and me, the book could quite easily be gone twenty or thirty years from now, when readers, not yet born, may spurn paper for the only thing they have ever known – pixels. We speak about 'digital natives' and 'digital immigrants' and say that anyone born after 1980 is a 'native'. This, to my mind, is nonsensical. The true digital natives have yet to be born and they will emerge in twenty or thirty years from now. The generation born between 1980 and 2040 may, in time, come to be known as the 'digital tourists'; not natives and not immigrants, but something in between. Not too dissimilar to the people of late eighteenth-century

---

[5] See Burke, *Literary Reading, Cognition and Emotion*; and Burke and Bon, 'Locations and Means', 205-232.

Britain, who, between approximately 1750 and 1800, had one foot still in the old agrarian-rural world and one foot in the new industrial-urban age.

The Reading Future

The plausible imminent demise of the paper book and the switch to reading digitally also throws up another important question: How long will human beings actually still be reading, and by default, writing too? Let me start this discussion with an anecdote. In 2018, I was teaching a short course to a small group of master's honours students in my university in Utrecht in the Netherlands. Approximately half the students were arts/humanities majors and half were science/technology majors. I split them into two groups and posed them the same question. The question was: 'How will we be reading 100 years from now, and why?' The arts/humanities students discussed the question among themselves and then explained to me that the reading landscape a hundred years from now would not be too dissimilar from what it is like today. We would still have a split between paper and pixels. There would be more digital reading but books would still be going very strong. Being a humanist scholar myself, this answer appealed to my cultural sensibilities on both a conscious and non-conscious level. Then I asked the science/technology honours students the same question. They answered immediately, almost with one voice, saying that 'one hundred years from now we will no longer be reading', adding, 'nor will we be writing'. They followed up by saying, 'Of course, there will be enthusiasts here and there who still read and write but it will be a bit like people today who have hobbies like knitting or embroidery'. One student added that maybe very traditional organisations like the church may still choose to read in public for performative persuasive reasons.

This answer shocked me and I went into automatic humanist denial. But shortly afterwards I started to reflect on it. I realised that just forty years ago there was no real internet; thirty years ago hardly anyone had an email address; twenty years ago many of the social media platforms that are taken for granted today – Facebook, Twitter, Instagram, and many others – didn't exist. Back in 1990, just thirty years ago, who could have imagined what reading and our digital lives could have looked like today? That was only thirty years ago and this prediction on reading that I put to my honours students was asking them to consider one hundred years from now. I drew two conclusions. The first was that the chance of things being more or less the same in one hundred years' time, as the arts/humanities students had predicted, was almost zero, barring some hugely destructive event like a thermo-nuclear world war, global pestilence, or a massive climate event that would stop the digital age in its tracks for a prolonged period. The second conclusion that I drew was that if we were unable to predict just how far digital technologies have come in the last thirty or forty years, how on earth can we predict with any certainty where these technologies might be in one hundred years' time? Indeed, might a hundred years in the digital age be more akin to two thousand years in the analogue age? In short, technological change is so fast moving that it is challenging to envision exactly what reading and writing will look like in 2120. However, we can perhaps creatively 'imagine' where it might go to, were it to disappear. The answer to the immediate future may very well lay in the past and in that key aspect of what makes us human: the rhetorical art of storytelling. Indeed, the near-future of reading could be auditory again and the near-future of writing once again oral in nature. This is because storytelling transcends the hardware and the skill of reading and writing. In effect, storytelling is a meta-level phenomenon of reading and writing.

We know the following: that technological innovation in a number of fields is moving toward a fuller integration of voice- and face-recognition solutions. The former of these, speech recognition, has been around since the 1970s, having been developed from the fields of linguistics, computer science, and artificial intelligence. Initially developed for people with manual disabilities, the technology has spread to numerous domains from healthcare to the military. Initially, the software had to be trained to learn the nature and idiosyncrasies of a given speaker's voice. Early programmes also had many errors in the output that needed repair. In the past five years, this technology has made a huge leap forward. Programmes can now become accustomed to a given voice almost immediately and there is a very low level of errors in the written output.

A case in point is in in-car sat-navigation systems, whereby manual input telling the computer what to do and where to go is quickly becoming obsolete in favour of voice input for the same functions. Another case is a product like Google smart speakers, whereby questions and commands can be posed orally at home, ranging from 'what time does my local supermarket close?' to 'is there a traffic jam on the Amsterdam ring road?' and the programme will answer you immediately drawing on its vast database of up-to-date knowledge. Writing, it would seem, and any manual creation of symbols to convey meaning, may be on its way out after 5,000 years: but what of its counterpart, reading?

We know that fewer and fewer younger people are reading to the extent that the generation before them did. A recent article in a leading Dutch newspaper reported that nowhere in broadly literate countries is reading for pleasure, digitally or otherwise, so low as it is in the Netherlands, where almost half of all fifteen year olds consider reading a literal waste of time.[6] Many other countries fared not much better than the Netherlands. We also know that the attention spans of young people are falling and that this is due to a significant extent to the amount of digital face-time they are

---

[6] See Mirjam Remnie and Patricia Veldhuis, 'Aap Noot Mis', *NRC*, February 1, 2020, 22-4, referring to the latest PISA study, a study conducted every three years among 600,000 school children across 77 countries.

engaging in in different domains, from reading to watching videos to gaming.

These days fewer parents are reading aloud to their younger children, and if they do they now have a number of alternative digital options. For example, busy parents can now record bedtime stories using the aforementioned Google smart speakers. A child need only switch on their tablet in bed and say, 'Hey Google, talk to My Storytime', and lo and behold the story starts. It will not be long before the computer can make the parent in this procedure obsolete by imitating the voice of the mother or father. In fact, the software is so fast at learning that parents are undoubtedly already redundant from a technological perspective. It is only the emotional idea of taking them out of the loop that is 'not done' that stops it being implemented right away.

Another development that needs our consideration is the audiobook developed many years ago and thought more or less redundant just twenty years ago. I have news: the audiobook is back, stronger than ever. A recent newspaper article in *The Times* shares that a Deloitte report, which includes figures from the 2019 annual technology and media trend predictions, has forecasted that the global audiobook market will grow by 25% to almost £4 billion in 2020. Crucially, in the United States, the world's largest market, audiobook revenues are on track to pass e-books by 2023. This is significant. It means that eyes may be replaced by ears in the domain of 'reading' much sooner than any of us dare imagine. The article describes how a better quality of sound in headphones, including the evolution of wifi, comfortable 'earbuds', and Apple's 'AirPods', is driving this change, along with the increasing number of celebrity readers who record books and authors who voice their own books.[7]

---

[7] Matthew Moore, 'Audiobook sales forecast to overtake e-books with revenue rising by 30 per cent', *The Times*, December 2, 2019.

An unmentioned, but to my mind significant, driver of this change must also be the cognitive ease that listening to a book offers compared to the cognitive effort that reading a book demands. Is the future of reading, listening? Well, quite plausibly, yes it is. This is the near future, but what about the distant future? What will the act of reading look like beyond 100 years, say, 500 or even 1,000 years from now? This is the realm of science fiction and is beyond the scope of this paper. Maybe virtual reality will lead and will be superseded by neural implants where stories could be directly downloaded thus bypassing the visual system. This is not as far-fetched as it may seem. Only last year Elon Musk announced that he was working on a brain-machine interface start-up called Neuralink involving wireless implantable devices that can ostensibly 'read the minds of others'.[8] This may very well be what the future will look like, but, in drawing this paper to a close, I would like us to reflect a little more deeply on the challenges of our reading present, brought about by the *in medias res* situation that reading finds itself in.

The Challenges of the Reading Present

Recent eye-tracking research into reading has shown that when we read on screens we skip through the text, zig-zagging our way from top to bottom in a kind of speed-reading mode. This is unlike reading from books (on paper) where readers tend to progress along the lines albeit with some regressions and fixations. Recent experiments have shown that reading behaviour in the digital condition can affect and influence reading behaviour in the book/paper condition; in short, that skipping through texts on digital screens makes us skip through texts when we read on paper. The major downside to this is that text comprehension levels are decreasing. A lack of knowing what a text says will almost certainly lead to a lack of knowing what a text means. This is a worry, as it may undermine

---

[8] Julie Carrie Wong, 'Elon Musk unveils plan to build mind-reading implants', *The Guardian*, July 17, 2019.

the citizen as a critical consumer of discourse and may leave the door open for a greater influence of state-actors on the general public in the malicious spread of fake news and post-truth 'realities'.[9] An upside of more screen-time reading is that boys, who have been notoriously poor book readers compared to girls, are now closing the gap owing to being able to engage with screens and smartphones instead of books. As the recent PISA study concludes, digital devices may be helping to improve the literacy of male teenagers.[10]

More generally, on the topic of literacy, there is a wider implication for the decline of reading and the resurgence of listening: an implication that has its positive sides in spite of our general scholarly and intellectual reservations. Although world literacy rates have increased significantly in the recent past, there are still huge swathes of the world where literacy rates remain low. One such region is sub-Saharan Africa, where the literacy rates in some countries are still below 30%.[11] A switch from reading to listening would eradicate this disadvantage almost immediately and lead to the building blocks of a level global playing field.

Yes, reading and writing may, in time, disappear. Humans managed without them before, 5,000 years ago, and they will probably do so again. What is here to stay, however, as long as humans are humans, is the emotive persuasive power of the rhetorical storyteller to tell tales and the emotive necessity for an audience to listen and in doing so be simultaneously both beguiled and instructed by those tales.

---

[9] See the work of the 'E-READ' group of researchers who between 2015 and 2018 investigated the future of reading and broadly concluded that 'the medium matters'. See also their 'The Stavanger Declaration on the Future of Reading' which also appeared in the *Frankfurter Allgemeine Zeitung* on January 22, 2019, https://www.faz.net/aktuell/feuilleton/buecher/themen/stavanger-erklaerung-von-e-read-zur-zukunft-des-lesens-16000793.html.

[10] Sian Griffiths, 'Smartphones and screens help boys close gap on girls in reading', *The Times*, November 3, 2019, citing the data from the 2019 PISA study.

[11] Max Roser and Esteban Ortiz-Ospina, 'Literacy', *OurWorldInData.org*, 2016, https://ourworldindata.org/literacy.

Conclusion

Speaking from an evolutionary perspective, reading is a very recent phenomenon. A question that can be posed: Is it a mere blip or will it stand the test of time? It is not easy for us to make that call. When you are in the middle of something that seems so normal and so natural and is so positive for education, for culture, for equality, it seems impossible that it could cease to exist.

This paper was primarily a reflection from a lover of books, but also from a bibliographic fossil on the edge of the precipice of time. It was a momentary observation in the year 2020, adrift in an undulating ocean of pixels and paper. Crucially, however, it was a reflection on the practice of reading in a state of flux. It is therefore unavoidable that you, the reader who may be reading this text in 2021 or later, will already be reading an outdated view of what was for me my 'reading reality'. For book lovers like myself, this tale may have been disturbing and confrontational. My general advice to any lover of books would be 'hold on to your hats' and enter into the immense changes that are undeniably to come with an open mind. Reading is about to write a new story in the coming years – and it will be one that will both delight and edify its listeners.

References

Benedetto, Simone, Véronique Drai-Zerbib, Marco Pedrotti, Geoffrey Tissier, and Thierry Baccino. 'E-readers and Visual Fatigue', *PloS one* 8, no. 12 (2013). DOI: 10.1371/journal.pone.0083676.

Burke, Michael and Esmeralda V. Bon. 'The Locations and Means of Literary Reading'. In *Expressive Minds and Artistic Creations: Studies in Cognitive Poetics*, ed. S. Csabi, 205-232. Oxford and New York: Oxford University Press, 2018.

Burke, Michael. *Literary Reading, Cognition and Emotion: An Exploration of the Oceanic Mind*. New York: Routledge, 2011.

Jeong, Hanho. 'A Comparison of the Influence of Electronic Books and Paper Books on Reading Comprehension, Eye Fatigue, and Perception'. *The Electronic Library* 30 (2012): 390–408. DOI: 10.1108/02640471211241663.

Siegenthaler, Eva, Laura Schmid, Michael Wyss, and Pascal Wurtz. 'LCD vs. E-ink: An Analysis of the Reading Behaviour'. *Journal of Eye Movement Research* 5, no. 5 (2012): 1–7.

Evolution of Reading in the Age of Digitisation (E-READ), 'The Stavanger Declaration on the Future of Reading', press release, January 22, 2019, https://ereadcost.eu/wp-content/uploads/2019/01/StavangerDeclarationPressRelease.pdf.

From Print to Pixels:
A Response to Michael Burke

Núria Bofarull Manzano

In his talk, Dr. Burke has posed as a central question: *How will we be reading one hundred years from now, and why?* In contemporary times, characterized by digital technology and mass visual culture, this question seems to become increasingly problematic. It is undeniable that the conditions imposed by the digital era have contributed to a shift in the way we understand heritage and its conservation. And not only heritage, but also the way in which we develop and share ideas, affecting the way we have always conceived written material. Furthermore – and perhaps the most remarkable aspect – is the fact that digital content is not necessarily embodied in physical or even material form, which will also intrinsically influence and transform our conception of the archive. In terms of publishing, the rise of digital forms of spreading knowledge has greatly contributed to a shift in the way we relate with printed publications. Besides, it seems that with the proliferation of digital content, the number of works that are worth being printed has become smaller and more selective. Consequently, a considerable amount of written text as well as other content will not reach a broader audience.

Through history we can see that in the Western tradition, before the revolution that came with printing, memory was understood as an essential tool for the transmission of culture, knowledge, and wisdom. They searched for ways of collecting ideas and efficiently recalling information. We could say that memory was seen as a huge storehouse. I find its conception as a palace particularly interesting. But then, I wonder: Instead of a palace for our memory, do we need a shelf or a library? And then, what happens when we move beyond that? When instead of a library we need cables? A connection.

In order to produce my response to this movement from the paper towards the pixel, I would like to propose an analogy with Plato's dialogue, *Theaetetus*. Essentially, this dialogue concerns the nature of knowledge. *'Similarly, being intelligent means having a large enough wax tablet to store lots of such impressions'.*[1] Plato compares human memory with a wax tablet. Memory relies on images fixed in the wax tablet of the mind. Memory then keeps these images and forgetting is a matter of losing them. In short, this dimension of knowledge is temporary. Our ability to store – collect and retain – information would be what measures our cognitive abilities. I would call it 'known-and-recollected knowledge'. In my contemporary reading, I would like to compare the wax tablet with the paper and the aviary with the pixel.[2]

Nowadays, however, books are not the main source of access to knowledge nor the only way to store and safeguard ideas. I like to see the ability to possess books as wax tablets that can contain a lot of impressions. Furthermore, because we have books, we do not rely entirely on our memory, as we saw in the examples from the beginning. So our dimension of knowledge is also temporary. We can always come back to the paper, to the pages of the book, to grasp its content. Because of its condition of physicality, the book stands and offers the possibility of being revisited.

Nowadays, we seem to be moving to the second model proposed by Plato, the aviary. That would be the pixel. We are going to call them 'known-but-not recollected knowledge' because they do not have a fixed location: They can simultaneously

---

[1] Plato, *Theaetetus* 194 c-d.
[2] According to the model proposed by Plato, the mind resembles an aviary full of birds where the possession of knowledge is comparable to a person who possesses birds in a cage (197C) where different birds represent different pieces of knowledge flying around in the aviary. A person has the power to activate any one of these pieces of knowledge by grasping one of the birds from their cage.

be reproduced in devices and they are constantly traveling.

While reading is present, the pixel is absent. I would like to illustrate my analogy with the aviary with a quote from Plato's *Theaetetus*:

> It is possible for someone to possess knowledge but not to hold it. As if some hunter should catch some wild birds and build them an aviary and keep them as pets at home. In one sense he holds them all the time, because he possesses them. In another sense he doesn't hold any of the birds. But he has got them under his control in a cage that belongs to him . . . so he has acquired a power over the birds to take hold of them and grasp them whenever he wants (197 c-d).

Pixels have the flying patterns of wild birds. Never before did we have access to such an amount of content even though it seems that at times our knowledge flickers like a bad internet connection. On the one hand, the rise of technology and the itinerancy of the pixel has enlarged the accessibility of knowledge and information. You can decide if you want to read Plato's dialogues from the printed pages of a book or on a device in an airplane. On the other hand, we seem to be overwhelmed by all these possibilities.

We are constantly exposed to screens, perhaps possessing knowledge instead of holding it, to stick to Plato's terms. In other words, scrolling instead of reading, and more interested in images than in words. I think it is hard to predict, at least from my humble perspective, how the future will look. I would like to finish my response considering an artwork called 'The Castle', by Jorge Méndez Blake. *(Fig. 1)*

A volume of Kafka's novel is inserted at the base of a brick wall, disrupting its structure. One of the readings we can make of

Fig. 1. The Castle, by Jorge Méndez Blake.

it is that ideas can have a great impact. Perhaps, in the future, due to the overexposure to screens and pixels we will regard printed material as a luxury and we will give it a high value with a strong desire to safeguard it. Thank you very much.

Objects of Empathy

Helle Hochscheid

Why is it important that we teach cultural heritage? Why is it important that we teach it, not just to willing victims who have more or less voluntarily wandered into our classrooms, but to the world at large? The question is one of more widely pressing importance than it would seem at first glance. If, as we believe, education about heritage, and I am referring in particular to archaeological heritage, is important, we cannot allow it to disappear from curricula; and to ensure that, we need to think about its meaning in the modern world. My paper, more than presenting you with an argument, will be an exploration of what heritage in education can achieve, and how it might do so.

A few years ago Peter Schultz presented a paper at a conference organized by the Beazley Archive, in which he shared some of the ideas of the historian and archaeologist, Robin Collingwood.[1] Collingwood's rather philosophical approach to history included a remarkable amount of archaeological practice, which he saw as instrumental in understanding the past. To quote the SEP:

> Genuine history seeks to recover the meaning behind the statements, not whether they are true or false (Haddock 1995). To recover such meanings historians must try, as far as possible, to bear in mind the epistemic and motivational premises of agents, even when they regard them as false. Thus an historian who comes across a statement claiming that certain agents changed their itinerary in order

---

[1] Peter's talk at https://podcasts.ox.ac.uk/collingwood-agency-and-archaeological-imagination-style-intention-late-classical-attic.

to avoid crossing mountains inhabited by devils, should not discard the statement as false but rather understand the decision making process in the light of the agent's beliefs, even if these are not shared by the historian.[2]

In contemporary historical practice this may seem like an open door, but Peter's reference to it reminded me of the fact that the opposite path is taken as often as not. For example, archaeologists have tried and do still try to match their evidence with models that, if all is well, they have based on a preliminary exploration of the first set of excavated material. While I admit that there is often little else to choose in making sense of scanty evidence, the component of human action in the material becomes generalized or possibly sidelined if the model is not flexible enough to accommodate the coincidences of lives past and present. And that can take away an essential opportunity offered by, in particular, archaeological or historical material: Such material, as most of you present here know, can make you feel the past, in a way that reading about it, or looking at it in a picture, cannot. And it is this capacity of archaeological heritage that lends it, in my view, special educational potential.

To explain what I mean by this capacity, let me make a slight detour through the work of Richard Sennett, an author of whom those of you who have developed the unfortunate habit of reading my work are probably already quite tired. In his 2013 book *Together*, Sennett elaborates on two classic forms of communication or conversation: dialectics and dialogics.[3] In a dialectic conversation – and sticking with Aristotle – the purpose is to convince your conversation partner of your view. To achieve that, the participants listen to each other, but also anticipate on their own

[2] https://plato.stanford.edu/entries/collingwood/.
[3] Sennett, *Together*, 18-20.

responses, thinking out their next move while the other is talking. In Sennett's view, this approach to communication encourages competition – if one person is convinced, the other person loses, in that their point of view is dismissed as of lesser value.

The other form of conversation is dialogics. The term was originally coined by the twentieth-century Russian literary theorist, Mikhail Bakhtin. In Sennett's description, dialogics are the empathetic form of conversed exchange: This means that while a person is listening to the other speaker, they are not thinking, 'how can I persuade this person of my view', but they are 'reading' what the other speaker means, not just on the level of the words, but also in the subtext, in inflections, in the tone of voice, in the body language.[4] This is necessary because the purpose of a dialogic conversation is not to win, or, to have your view on a matter completely changed into the other person's, but to jointly reach a new insight, new common ground that is the result of giving and taking on both sides. To do this successfully, planning your next lines in your head is not useful. Instead, it is key to closely read the communication as it comes to you, hearing specifics in it, and to be able to put yourself in the other person's shoes.[5] In other words, dialogics require empathetic taking in of the offered communication. Their reward is a deeper understanding of what is being communicated and why it is thus communicated.

Back to heritage, and in particular archaeological heritage. In recent years, the ways in which humans and objects interact have been the subject of increasing scholarship. Some aspects of this research draw on the work of Bourdieu or of earlier scholars: They acknowledge that objects, whether they are tangible things or practices, have a constructive and creative role in self-identification

---

[4] Sennett, 19, cf. 20-21.
[5] Sennett, 20.

and self-differentiation.[6] Differently put, people define who they are in interaction with everyday objects. Material culture's *'ability (...) to implicitly condition human actions becomes the primary means by which people are socialized'*.[7] In recent years, more layers have been added to this view of materiality. For example, the archaeologist Ian Hodder expounds how *'Our thinking comes about as an interaction between brain and world'*.[8] As examples, he gives our use of the external world to jog our thinking, for instance, when we prompt our neural pathways through rearranging Scrabble tiles over and over to find that word that will fit, or when we work out in our head a complex sum using the same method we would apply if we had pen and paper to do it. Humans, Hodder and others have argued, think in embodied practical ways.[9] They solve problems wonderfully and creatively, and always have: and they particularly have always done so in situational contexts. Ask yourself, if I had a nail but no hammer, how would I get the nail into a board? The fact that you could in all likelihood come up with a solution, gives you a glimpse of the capacity of your brain to *think with things*.

The way such thinking with things is achieved is this: The answers to our questions are in the parts of the problem. To hammer in a nail without a hammer, you need to find an alternative object that can serve that purpose, or, you can try chiseling a hole with your nail (although a screw would then be better – so you can try to exchange the nail for a screw), etc. While problems that we pose to students in classes are usually theoretical problems, the question is whether we would not do better to also stimulate the ability to solve problems on this object-cognitive level. Our strengths seem to be, historically, or perhaps, archaeologically, in that area.

---

[6] Miller, *Materiality*.
[7] Miller, 6.
[8] Hodder, *Entangled*, 35-36.
[9] Hodder, 37.

And here, another element comes in. In education, certainly at university level, the immaterial takes precedence over the material. Where in the past, education was more often than not grounded in material practice and included apprenticeships or learning practices from family, in universities this has declined in favor of immaterial contemplation.[10] Recently, there seems to be a change of heart, and it might be wise to follow this trend. Because education as it is, favoring theory over things, setting learning outcomes that are often dialectic and grades that establish hierarchy, is missing out. While these things are undeniably useful and sometimes necessary, the present day greatly needs another, different set of skills, as other contributions to this volume also bring into the limelight. So the question is how the material, how things, could be brought into academic education meaningfully, and how it could help build and grow creative problem-solving abilities.

There is an assignment in my introduction to archaeology class, taught in the context of the arts and humanities department of a Liberal Arts and Sciences college. Students get small archaeological objects, some reproductions, some 'real'. They have to describe the object without saying what they think it is (this sometimes leads to hilarious guesses), then give the description to a fellow student who has to draw what they described, without having seen the object in the description, based purely on the text. While this usually leads to much amusement in the class (never a bad thing), what it mainly does is trigger students' ability to solve problems. What is this object? How old is it? What is it made of? Since at that point in the course they do not know anything yet about chronology, archaeological classification, style development, or periodization, the exercise is instinctive. It becomes about sensing, watching, smelling, holding; it becomes about reading an object that you do not completely get.

---

10 Miller, 6-7.

To do this exercise well, you have to listen to the object; you have to read it and feel it; and you have to refrain from imposing preconceived ideas onto it.

In other words, you have to let the object into your mind, just as it is. Students tend to do this remarkably well. They practice dialogics – on a Chinese cricket holder or a reproduction ancient Greek rattle. In some ways, objects are like people, and this is what makes it possible to have a dialogic conversation with them.[11] But it does more than that: because our brains sense objects in an embodied way, practicing dialogics on a thing or a person is more similar that it would seem. While observing an object that they do not know the function of, students' brains perform simulated scenarios of use, as their senses process the physical qualities of the object. In a slightly different form, trained archaeologists do this every day: They sense the object, ask it questions, read it, and listen to it. And it is my contention that honing this ability to think with things, can improve dialogic skills.

Critical listening or critical reading of the object, exchange or experience with it, is probably what many archaeologists love about their job.[12] It certainly is what I love about it. But it can be so much more. Heritage should be taught in classrooms through itself. Objects should loom large in academic education. Why? Because the mind thinks with things – and thinking with things well helps you think with other people. To paraphrase Daniel Miller: We need to teach how the things that people make, make people.

---

[11] See further, for instance, Ingold, *Making*; Malafouris, *How Things Shape*.
[12] As eloquently confirmed by Knappett, *An Archaeology of Interaction*, 3-14.

References

Hodder, Ian. *Entangled. An Archaeology of the Relationships between Humans and Things*. London: Wiley-Blackwell, 2012.

Ingold, Tim. *Making. Anthropology, Archaeology, Art and Architecture*. London: Routledge, 2013.

Knappett, Carl. *An Archaeology of Interaction. Network Perspectives on Material Culture and Society*. Oxford: Oxford University Press, 2011.

Malafouris, Lambros. *How Things Shape the Mind. A Theory of Material Engagement*. Cambridge: MIT Press, 2013.

Miller, Daniel, ed. *Materiality*. Durham: Duke University Press, 2005.

Sennett, Richard. *Together. The Rituals, Pleasures and Politics of Cooperation*. London: Penguin Books, 2013.

Connecting with Things Through The Senses: A Call For A Multi-Sensory Museum Experience

Sien Christiaanse & Artemisia Loesberg

We are lucky enough to be in Helle's class ourselves. Her talk reminded us of some interesting points that were brought up during this course. Helle brought diverse and particularly strange objects to the classroom, and we were asked to act like the curators of our own exhibition. In this way, we were challenged to engage with material culture in a different way. We developed the idea of letting the visitors choose an object that spoke to them. They could freely interact with it, and afterwards they would take the object and walk to one of our colleagues who would interpret the object for them with a quirky fortune-telling perspective.

Fig 1. In-class curation assignment.

One of the things that struck us when looking back on this exercise was the way we set up the space, especially the way we used the whiteboard. We drew an image of a finger raised to your lips – a gesture meant to indicate 'be silent' – and the words 'respect the museum' were drawn on the board. *(Fig. 1)* This connects to the imposed silence of the museum culture which we elaborately discussed in class, and will touch upon later in this response.

With our exhibition, we wanted to explore a non-conventional way to engage with material culture, a way that engages more with what is behind the glass. As visitors, we desire to establish a certain connection with the artefact, one that is fueled by our emotions and willingness to learn.[1] In a way, museum culture restricts this desire for a deep, meaningful connection by isolating objects behind glass displays, imposing a rule of silence or whispers. In addition, the interaction is often merely through one or two senses, while overlooking the potential of all five sensory organs.

We understand that the vulnerability of these objects restricts museums, and that the conservation and preservation of the object has to be prioritised. However, opening up this discussion offers the possibility for a more complete and meaningful interaction. This has the potential to open up the museum to a wider range of people, an audience that goes beyond the static, traditional, rather homogeneous audience.[2]

One of the reasons museums tend to emphasize vision in their exhibitions is what Viv Golding calls the 'eye-minded philosophy of the West'.[3] This refers to the Western model that places vision at the top of the hierarchy, hearing slightly below, and taste, touch, and smell at the bottom. During the course we discussed how museums might not work in non-Western contexts, and we propose that the focus on this Western model of the senses is part of that. If we attempt to include more senses and thus more ways of engaging with the material – the objects – this will appeal to a wider audience and you will be able to educate people more efficiently.

Furthermore, this hierarchy could be argued to be a racist one; Jo Day, for instance, argues that when Europeans were brought into contact with peoples seen as primitive, these peoples were expected to show a natural predilection for the 'lower' senses of taste, touch, and smell.[4] Hamilakis asserts that otherness is defined

[1] Smith, 'Theorizing Museum and Heritage Visiting', 460.
[2] Black, 'Meeting the Audience Challenge', 1.
[3] Dudley, *Museum Materialities*, 225.
[4] Day, *Making Senses of the Past*, 4.

partly by a particularly negative odour.[5] He further discusses how Europeans attempted to 'civilize' the non-European 'other' by, amongst other methods, deodorising them.[6] We discussed in the course how even when museums attempt to be diverse, and include non-Western themes for exhibitions, there is this sense of otherness that partly defeats the purpose. Therefore, it is interesting that through the senses – or undervaluing some senses and overvaluing others – this process of othering also occurs. The value that Western museums place on a visual experience of the artefacts, especially if these artefacts originate from non-Western cultures, can be seen to disregard the origins and function of said artefact. Their 'use' becomes subordinate to their visual appeal and preservation; they are seen as isolated from their function, and consequently isolated from the sensory experience that is associated with their function.[7]

We would like to give some examples of the ways in which museums tend to focus on the visual and the aural. Firstly, in an exhibition at the National Museum of Antiquity in Leiden, the Netherlands, 'Cyprus: A Dynamic Island', a common way to contextualize the artefacts was through the display of quote texts. (Fig. 2) A sign shows a quote from the Iliad, which stimulates a different engagement with the

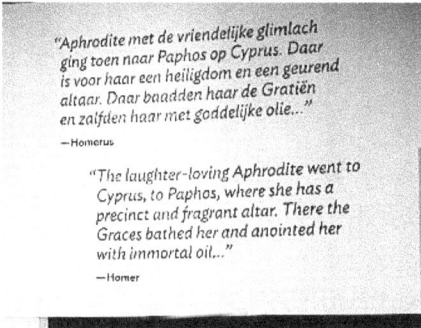

"Aphrodite met de vriendelijke glimlach ging toen naar Paphos op Cyprus. Daar is voor haar een heiligdom en een geurend altaar. Daar baadden haar de Gratiën en zalfden haar met goddelijke olie..."
—Homerus

"The laughter-loving Aphrodite went to Cyprus, to Paphos, where she has a precinct and fragrant altar. There the Graces bathed her and anointed her with immortal oil..."
—Homer

Fig. 2. Artemisia Loesberg / Courtesy of Museum of Antiquity, 'Cyprus: A Dynamic Island'.

ancient artefacts for the visitor; it puts the visitor on a certain track of

---

[5] Hamilakis, Archaeology and the Senses, 18.
[6] Hamilakis, 18.
[7] Ahmed, What's the Use?, 33.

thought. Instead of asking the audience to engage merely with the artefacts, it asks the audience to think about the culture these objects are placed in and thus about how the artefact would not have been isolated but would have been part of a bigger picture.

Fig. 3. Artemisia Loesberg/ Courtesy of Drents Museum, 'Sprezzatura'.

A different approach is taken at the Drents Museum's 'Sprezzatura', one that has an emphasis on the aural sense. This exhibition on Italian paintings provides the option of listening to recordings of Italian plays that were influential in the same period in which the paintings were created. (Fig. 3) It leads to a different experience for the visitor which affects the way they engage with the other objects in the room.

Noise is a funny thing in museums. In a traditional museum, it is only allowed to exist in a particular, restricted, and controlled way, as seen in the last example. These same restrictions did not apply to the forerunner of the museum: the cabinets of curiosity established in the Enlightenment. Objects were allowed to be touched and heated discussions about these artefacts were central to the experience. It is barely imaginable, but the noise seemed to be a prominent part of the museum culture. Indeed, this dynamic interaction might have been encouraged.

A second point is that this reliance on vision is imposed by the museum. We have three illustrations of this. The first photo is to show that the glass, rope, or any separation automatically forces any visitor to rely on vision rather than touch or smell. (Fig. 4)

In the second photo, you can see an Angisa, a headscarf, an artefact made of cloth; cloth is a material that increases the tendency to interact with the object through touch. *(Fig. 5)* The headscarf is similar to the third photo, a piece of clothing, something we engage with every day, which seems to invite touch yet is barred from the visitor behind glass. *(Fig. 6)* This is not to say that visitors should always be free to touch objects, but simply that forcing this reliance on vision changes the interaction with the object. By expanding the experience to more senses, a deeper and more meaningful connection could be established.

Furthermore, we would like to include several examples of multi-sensory initiatives and exhibitions. The first is 'Inspiration Africa!', which was a programme jointly managed by the Horniman Museum and the Cloth of Gold arts company, and which engaged twelve schools in twelve object-based projects. Viv Golding was the outreach worker for the Brent Knoll school, and the students she worked with were all on the autistic spectrum. These students were offered the opportunity to engage in tactile experiences with a restricted range of original objects from the West African handling collection. Golding mentions

Fig. 4. Artemisia Loesberg/ Metal bar keeping viewers away from 'Het Ongeloof van Thomas', Courtesy of Rijksmuseum, Amsterdam.

Fig. 5. Artemisia Loesberg/ Courtesy of The Museum of the Tropics, 'Angisa'.

Fig. 6. Artemisia Loesberg/ Courtesy of Musée de l'Armée, 'Military Costume'.

how two non-verbal students especially enjoyed smelling one of the objects. This shows how one of the least-appreciated senses, smell, can actually be essential for some people in their interaction with objects.

The Prado Museum in Madrid offers another example of a museum

Fig. 7. Multi-sensory display, Ignacio Hernando Rodriguez / Courtesy of Prado Museum.

including other senses than vision. In fact, their initiative called 'Touching the Prado' was focused on the visually impaired. It included 3D copies of six works that were representative of varying pictorial genres, which visitors were allowed to touch. The display also included material such as texts in braille, audio guides, and opaque glasses aimed at facilitating the experience for fully sighted visitors. *(Fig. 7)*

Fig. 8. Artemisia Loesberg / Courtesy of Touching Different Material, Museum of Antiquity.

Finally, the Museum of Antiquity in Leiden attempted to include multiple senses. One of them is touch; they offered a possibility to feel the difference between marble, bronze, and plaster. *(Fig. 8)*

These examples show how museums can integrate different senses in the experiences they offer and there are several advantages to changing a museum experience into such a multi-sensory experience. Firstly, we notice that these different approaches include visitors that are mostly marginalised from the average audience, such as autistic children or the visually impaired; it no longer bars these people from the museum experience. Moreover, people learn through various senses and interact with the world in various ways, which is why a multi-sensory museum experience is more effective in appealing to people as well as educating them. Finally, it offers a more complete interaction with these objects.

We also used an experiment to further demonstrate how our sensory organs might influence the way you perceive and think about objects. We had several objects for this: two Artemis statuettes, a decorated (empty) perfume oil flask, and an old newspaper article. In addition, we invited a Turkish musician to play traditional music. This was to give the audience the possibility to interact with all their senses; they could touch their objects, smell them (in the case of the perfume oil, flask, and the old newspaper), and listen to the music.

The objects were given to random members in the audience, some of whom were also given gloves and earplugs. They first had to interact with the object with gloves on, or earplugs in, and then were allowed to interact without the gloves and earplugs. This was to test if their experience would be different if they could interact with the object using more senses.

The participants confirmed the different experiences of the artefacts; when listening to the music they admitted having a particularly unique experience with the objects. This was also the case when the sensory organs were triggered through smell and tactile sensations.

We suggest changing museum culture by working towards an engagement of all five sensory organs and lifting some of the restrictions museums impose. For example, encouraging people to actually discuss the objects on display, rather than enforcing the established whisper culture, could lead to dialogues not just between the visitors, but between visitors and objects. Certainly, we want to protect these objects from accidental destruction, but we also want to protect them from isolated lives where there is no dialogue.

References

Ahmed, Sara. *What's the Use?: On the Uses of Use*. Durham: Duke University Press, 2019.

Black, Graham. 'Meeting the Audience Challenge in the 'Age of Participation''. *Museum Management and Curatorship* 33, no. 4 (2018): 302-319.

Day, Jo. *Making Senses of the Past: Toward a Sensory Archaeology*. Carbondale: Southern Illinois University Press, 2013.

Dudley, Sandra, ed. *Museum Materialities. Objects, Engagements, Interpretations*. London: Routledge, 2010.

Hamilakis, Yannis. *Archaeology and the Senses: Human Experience, Memory, and Affect*. New York: Cambridge University Press, 2014.

Smith, Laurajane. 'Theorizing Museum and Heritage Visiting'. In *Museum Theory*, edited by Andrea Witcomb and Kylie Message, 459-84. Vol. 1 of *The International Handbooks of Museum Studies*. New York: Wiley, 2015.

Teaching Arabic Like the Classics:
Inspiration for Employability

Emily Selove

Introduction

Because of events occurring in the Middle East over the past decades, awareness grows amongst Western universities and their students of the 'strategic' value of knowledge of the Arabic language. The military and economic implications of the word 'strategic' here are obvious, and perhaps distasteful to those of us who are ear-deep in Arabic literature, and therefore see the Arabic language as valuable because it is one of the most important and influential literary languages in the history of the human race.[1]

The West's difficult relationship with this obvious fact has long been tied up with its often difficult relationship with Arabic-speaking countries. Let us take medical literature as an example: Medical literature is one area where medieval Arabic-speaking writers were so influential that even those otherwise oblivious of medieval Arabic literature can recognise names like Avicenna (Ibn Sīna, d. 1037) and Averroes (Ibn Rushd, d. 1198). Although Arabic medical and philosophical texts continued to influence Europe during the Renaissance and beyond, Renaissance authors used Arabs as the foil against which to define themselves, as demonstrated, for example, in this quote by Leonard Fuchs (d. 1566):

> It is best to sideline and simply reject the Arab authors, the barbarians of a bygone age, and learn—
> as if drawing water from the purest sources—from

---

[1] For example, see Jaschik, 'Millions for Strategic Languages'.

the writings of Greek physicians . . . Just as in the teachings of the Arabs all is dirty, barbarous, filthy, complicated, and riddled with the most horrendous errors, all things Greek are clean, clear, shining, brilliant, open, and uncontaminated by any error.[2]

As has been famously demonstrated by Edward Said in his influential work *Orientalism,* Europe often painted the Arabs as the despicable and exotic Other. And in spite of the fact that Arabic writing could be considered as influential in the development of European civilization as that of the ancient Greeks and Romans, and that the Arab world could be considered as much the heir of Classical civilization as Europe, Europe claimed these Classical civilisations as its ancestors and held them up as the source of European superiority over the Middle East and other regions. This is all pertinent when we consider teaching Arabic like the Classics, as demonstrated below.

The pedagogical picture is further complicated by the diglossia of the Arabic language. The language of high literature is distinct from the colloquial languages spoken in Arabic-speaking countries. Medieval Arabists such as myself are therefore faced with a kind of dilemma: We often serve students who are interested in learning more about current events in Arabic-speaking countries and in speaking to Arabic-speaking people. To learn more about current events, students often wish to read Arabic-language newspapers, which use a type of formal Arabic (Modern Standard Arabic) that is similar to, but still different from, the language of the Qur'an and of the great works of medieval Arabic literature. To speak to Arabic-speaking people, students need to learn one of many dialects, which are all very different from the language of medieval Arabic literature. And by acquiring knowledge of Modern Standard and colloquial

---

[2] Savage-Smith and Pormann, *Medieval Islamic Medicine*, 169.

Arabic, students often hope to gain employment in, for example, the military, journalism, or businesses with interests in the Middle East.

But by focusing on these skills to the exclusion of the language of the Qur'an and of medieval Arabic literature, students are missing out on something crucial about the Arabic language – namely that it is, as stated above, one of the most important and influential literary languages in the history of the human race. Ancient Greek and Latin are universally acknowledged in Western universities as languages that were home to literary traditions that profoundly influenced the world we live in today. Arabic equally deserves this recognition. For a Western student of Arabic to graduate without a personal appreciation of this fact is more than a tragic missed opportunity; it effaces the contributions of the Arabic language to human culture by reducing this language to a tool of strategic military and economic value.

Nevertheless, the question of employability remains a problem. Students are not going to get hired by oil companies because of their profound appreciation of al-Jāḥiẓ and Abū Nuwās (names I wish were as immediately recognisable to English-speaking readers as those of Herodotus and Catullus).[3] This paper will seek to explain how such an appreciation can, however, improve a student's employability. In the above paragraph, I compared the literary importance of Arabic to that of ancient Greek and Latin; the field of Classics has done a lot of work to demonstrate the importance of the skills acquired by a student of Classics to gaining employment, and I will draw on this work in this essay. I will also offer some thoughts on teaching the Arabic language as a language of literary importance.

---

[3] Al-Jāḥiẓ (d. 868) is remembered as the 'father of Arabic prose', who wrote on an enormously wide range of topics, both lofty and quotidien. Abū Nuwās (d. 814) is perhaps the most famous Arabic poet, known for his verses about wine and beautiful young men who serve the wine.

Arabic and the Classics

There are plenty of reasons to study medieval Arabic in much the same way that we study ancient Greek and Latin. Three main reasons will be briefly covered here: First, ancient Greek (and, to a lesser degree, Latin) literature is intimately related to medieval Arabic literature. Second, until fairly recently, classical Arabic was studied in much the same way as the Classics, and although this mode of study was motivated in part by outdated assumptions, we need not throw the baby out with the bathwater in updating these methods. And finally, in reclaiming these methods and re-examining our perspective on the relationship of Arabic and the Classics, we can in fact address many of the concerns and interests of our students wishing to engage with the modern Middle East.

It will not be possible in this brief essay to touch on all of the many ways that medieval Arabic literature was formative to the culture of Europe. Leonard Fuchs goes on to say (after the quote cited above), 'The Arabs have nothing that they did not take from . . . the Greeks, apart from the errors which are typical of them'. Suffice it to say that this is a myth which persists to this day, and which has everything to do with a prejudiced, Orientalist attitude on the matter, and which is emphatically false. Moreover, the influences of Arabic literature on European literature extended well beyond the generally recognised contributions in medicine, philosophy, and certain branches of the sciences such as astronomy and optics, and included profound influences on material culture as well as poetry and prose writing that helped develop the modern novel. Furthermore, as stated above, medieval Arabic literature is every bit as much the heir to Classical civilisation as is the literature of Europe. The Hellenization of the medieval Middle East can be seen not only in its interest in medicine, astronomy/astrology, and philosophy, but also in its wine and banquet literature, its hagiography, its traditions of rhetorical literary debate, and much more.

Since Adam Mez (d. 1917) reframed Arabists' interest in the language as a study pertinent to the field of Classics, as opposed to the fields of Biblical studies and theology, medieval Arabic was taught in much the same way as a Classical language – that is to say, students learned to read the formal language with a dictionary, focusing on medieval texts. More recently, attention has turned to 'media Arabic' and the spoken dialects, probably partly out of distaste for the outdated Orientalist attitudes that accompanied the old style of reading Arabic, which often held the language up to the standard of ancient Greek and Latin with the implicit assumption that it was an inferior, decadent development of these Classical traditions.

We now have the opportunity to reclaim these methods by making the Classics not the measuring stick that Arabic fails to measure up to, but the equal of Arabic as a language of importance to Western culture. Such methods can be used in conjunction with instruction on media Arabic and spoken Arabic to provide students with a more complete picture of the richness and significance of their language of study. Moreover, teaching students of Arabic techniques used in the study of the Classics increases their employability, as shown in the following section.

Employability and the Classics

There are two ways to think about teaching Arabic like the Classics. The first is to teach students the historical and cultural significance of pre-modern Arabic literature, and the ability to read, analyse, and research this literature. Those are the skills discussed in this section. The next section will offer some thoughts on the pedagogical implications of teaching the formal written Arabic language in much the same way as you might teach Latin or ancient Greek.

Students anxious about their employment prospects might see the analysis of ancient and medieval literature as an irrelevant waste of time. As a lecturer in medieval Arabic literature, this attitude naturally hurts my feelings, but it is important to recognise the students' very real concerns about their financial future. The fact is, employers value the skills gained by students well-versed in historical and literary studies, and it is important to tell the students that this is the case, so that they know to showcase their skills in their cover letters and their job interviews.[4]

The University of Exeter's Classics department has this to say about employability:

> A degree in Classics and Ancient History will provide you with skills which are highly valuable to employers across many sectors. You will develop an advanced knowledge of other cultures, learning how to think logically and independently, to interpret and critique sources, to assess and evaluate information and to communicate in a sophisticated way.
>
> Six months after graduating, 91.9%* of our Classics and Ancient History students are employed or in further study.[5]

---

[4] 'Whatever you do, it is crucial that students are able to see what the link is between course elements or distinct employability activities and achievements that employers will value. They need to have the language and confidence to demonstrate what they have learned on their CVs, in job applications, in interviews and in meetings with potential employers at job fairs, conferences and elsewhere', 'Improving Student Employability', 8.
[5] https://www.exeter.ac.uk/undergraduate/degrees/classics/careers/.

As a lecturer in the Institute of Arab and Islamic Studies, I can benefit from these formulations of the Classics department in reassuring students who may be interested in studying literature but who are concerned about employment. If such students also have the skills gained in, for example, a degree in politics, this only increases their range of desirable skills.

Because a Classics degree is more common than a degree in medieval Arabic literature, there are many more resources devoted to explaining to students how such a degree could improve their employability. These resources are equally applicable to students interested in medieval Arabic literature. For example, an online resource devoted to helping students think about their career prospects has this to say about employability skills gained in a Classics degree:

> You will develop the ability to research, collate and analyse materials, including written documentation and statistics. You will also learn to critically evaluate and interpret resources in order to formulate impartial and coherent arguments, which you can present competently in both the spoken and written word.[6]

It may seem obvious that these are useful skills gained from studying most historical and literary sources, but it may not be obvious to students that describing their literary research projects that demonstrated these skills could make them stand out to a potential employer.

---

[6] See https://www.prospects.ac.uk/careers-advice/what-can-i-do-with-my-degree/classics. *The Guardian* published a similar article helping students understand how their Classics degree might help them find employment: Scott, 'What to Do with a Degree in Classics'.

To this general list of skills outlined in the quotations above, the University of Durham's history department also emphasizes the value of an 'appreciation of the validity of the views of others'.[7]

In the Institute of Arab and Islamic Studies, we recently jointly composed a document titled 'Integrated Vision of Educational Excellence and Education Strategy: IAIS 2017'. It had this to say on employability and the importance of appreciating the views of others:

> The degrees offered by the IAIS provide a means for students to acquire specialized regional knowledge while also developing the intellectual skills and qualities of mind associated with achievement of a BA with honours in arts, humanities and social sciences subjects. By giving prominence to the distinctiveness and significance of specific areas and fostering a critical awareness of diversity across societies both past and present, the IAIS (as an area studies department) has a particular contribution to make in the context of increasingly multicultural societies... The programmes offered at the IAIS encourage students to develop a strong sense of perspective and flexibility in thinking, and graduates are well attuned to diversity. All of these qualities have strong employer appeal in an increasingly globalized world, in which the possession of intercultural competences and relevant language skills has never been more important.

Debate has raged over the last decade over whether the humanities

---

[7] https://www.dur.ac.uk/history/undergraduate/career_options/.

have to be 'useful', as pressure increases on humanities departments to prove their relevance to the economy. Protestations that the humanities have an intrinsic value irrelevant to their economic significance often focus on skills mentioned in this section – namely, that they help students think critically, express themselves, and appreciate the views of others. As it turns out, these intrinsically valuable skills are also skills that improve a student's earning power. This will be addressed further in the conclusion, but first, I will briefly consider some pedagogical questions related to language teaching which are largely unique to the Arabic language.

A Word on Arabic Language Teaching

Suzanne Stetkevych's article, 'Observations on Arabic language teaching', gives an excellent overview of the history of Arabic language teaching in the United States (also applicable to the UK), explaining how a declining interest in elite education and its focus on the Classics in the post-World War II era has contributed to a growing interest in practical, conversational instruction in the Arabic language. Without a knowledge of grammatical structures and terminologies, however, which were traditionally learned by students of Greek and Latin, language instructors are left without a common vocabulary to teach such concepts to their students, who have never studied the grammar of even the English language. Stetkevych writes:

> To have to devote hours of precious class time to teaching English grammar as a basis for understanding Arabic grammar is indeed onerous, but I'm not sure there is any escape. In my experience, the non-grammatical teaching approach and the idea that students can be taught comprehension techniques of strategies

for guessing meanings of words and structures reaches a crisis point after the first two years.[8]

This is exactly the point at which I take up instruction of the intermediate Arabic language students of the Institute of Arab and Islamic Studies at the University of Exeter. And because I was myself trained in a rather old-school fashion in both Arabic and Latin, with all the accompanying vocabulary, I have found it difficult at times to communicate with my students on the subject of Arabic grammar. The following student evaluation bluntly expresses some (though not all) of my students' reactions to my attempts to teach using the Arabic grammar books that my professors used to teach me:

> Even the most basic grammar points which we have known for the last 3 years are made excessively convoluted and complicated by obscure and obsolete terms. The context in which we learn grammar is classical Arabic and the vocabulary used fails to seem relevant to those of us who want to communicate with modern Arabs.

Some examples of the 'obscure and obsolete' terms to which the student objects include words like predicate, and participle, as well as terms especially associated with the study of Greek and Latin, like nominative, accusative, and genitive. Although I am, at the time of writing this essay, thirty-three years old, it appears that I am already a dinosaur for considering these words to be part of the necessary vocabulary for a student of language.

In recognition of this fact, I am in the process of changing my strategy. As Stetkevych notes in her essay, the tendency of Arabic

---

[8] Stetkevych, 'Observations', 16-17.

students today is to approach a text in an impressionistic way, guessing vaguely at its meaning without much attention to the details of the morphology and grammar of a word or phrase. This is a useful and necessary method to gain a quick first impression of a text, and it is often best not to get too bogged down on a difficult word or phrase that could discourage a student from tackling a difficult passage at large. It is necessary, however, to convey to students the skills needed to slow down their reading and dissect a passage piece by piece, taking into account the information conveyed by each prefix, suffix, and morphological pattern. This is a skill as essential to the translator of modern Arabic as it is to the scholar of medieval Arabic. I have concluded that it is hopeless to convey this information in the traditional method of language instruction, and have opted for a hands-on approach that involves questions about specific words or phrases in a reading passage, questions which are designed to help a student understand how they can skillfully and precisely translate such a passage on their own using a dictionary. A satisfied student reports of this new, hands-on approach to philological training:

> A massive improvement on last year. It can be safely said that no one expected to ever learn some of the vocabulary that we have covered through medieval text analysis – however, this has been an engaging way of using grammatical analysis as a tool to aid in developing understanding.

This new hands-on approach also offers opportunities to design 'authentic' assessment options, where a grammar student, instead of, for example, filling in a verb chart, would answer questions about a reading passage that would demonstrate more real-life skills of an Arabist facing a difficult text.

The diglossia of the language is another thorny problem that frankly has not been solved by the Arabic language teaching community, and is too large a problem to be effectively addressed in this short essay.[9] Suffice it to say that scholars of medieval Arabic literature are not always equipped to instruct students on the art of 'communicating with modern Arabs' (as the above disgruntled evaluation puts it) and therefore we need more urgently to address the perceived relevance of our expertise to the job prospects of our young students. This I have attempted to do with the previous section on employability and the Classics, but the question must also be considered within the wider context of the struggle of all university humanities departments to prove their relevance to the modern economy. This question is addressed in the following section.

Conclusion: Do the Humanities Have to be Useful?

Like many medievalists, my love for my subject of study sprang from a love for the esoteric and strange, and for reading dusty old books in a quiet corner. I have often been reluctant to find myself, as an Arabist, suddenly thrust into the spotlight and considered relevant to current events in the Arabic-speaking world. I had mixed feelings, for example, when my translation of an 11th-century book about gate-crashing was featured on BBC radio and in several prominent newspapers and magazines, supposedly for proving that Muslims could be funny and enjoy a good wine-drinking party as much as anyone else.[10] Although I was flattered by the attention, the problems inherent in this claim are too numerous to mention; imagine if we used Chaucer to prove that English people (English people today and for all time) like to go on long trips and tell dirty

---

[9] See Owens, 'The Grammatical Tradition'; Ryding, *Teaching and Learning Arabic*; and Younes 'Integrating', for three different viewpoints on the subject.
[10] For example, the 2012 BBC World Update interview can be found here: https://soundcloud.com/inqualitymedia/dr-emily-selove-from-the. Also see, 'Medieval Guide to Party-Crashing in Iraq reveals 'Different' Islam', http://www.bbc.co.uk/news/uk-england-manchester-20509649.

stories. Of course it would be correct. It would also be an outrageous argument.

I have gradually reached the conclusion that a knowledge of the importance of medieval Arabic literature, its enormous variety, its influence on Western culture, and its relatability and humanity (*humans* in general like parties and dirty jokes), is essential to understanding the modern world and challenging the often Orientalist or racist discussions in which we are all immersed. But my struggle with this question reflects a larger struggle occurring within universities over the past few decades – a struggle summed up well in the volume of short essays titled, *Do the Humanities Have to be Useful?*

This question was posed at Cornell University in 2006 in the face of a challenge to the humanities to prove their value to the modern economy. Naturally the first reaction to such a challenge is to protest that literature and art make human life worth living; what could be more valuable than that? But since few people make money writing poetry, we must struggle to express, as I have in this essay, that skills acquired in the humanities can, for example, help a student to obtain gainful employment.

Ross Brann's contribution to the volume, 'An Area Studies Perspective', is the most relevant to the topic at hand, because it focuses on humanities conducted within Near Eastern Studies departments. He writes: 'From the vantage point of area studies in general and Near Eastern Studies in particular, to question the usefulness of the humanities seems altogether superfluous'.[11] It is patently obvious that a knowledge of the language and culture of the Middle East is 'useful'. Brann goes on to explain that area studies facilitate interdisciplinary conversations, and that scholars

---

[11] Brann, 'Area Studies Perspective', 8.

of the pre-modern Middle East are especially well placed to encourage such conversations because pre-modern scholars were not themselves constrained by modern disciplinary boundaries, but were often polymaths, at once poets and scientists, for example.[12] By encouraging conversation across disciplinary and cultural boundaries, he suggests, we may encourage such interactions beyond the classroom, fostering the cooperation necessary for a healthy society and economy.

But the humanities can contribute in other ways to our economy. For example, Carolyn Martin, professor of German Studies and president of Amherst College, argues that just as the importance of innovation in technology is emphasised in our rapidly changing world, we should also seek flexible, innovative, and creative thinking in our culture and language:

> The humanities, at their best, are a celebration of transport, transformation, and wonder. The work of critique, no less than of the creative arts, enables thought, discovery, and insight by ridding us of the rigidities and exhausted forms that kill curiosity and limit us to our fears. We place enormous hope as a nation in technological innovation and the sciences that drive it, as we should. Let us put as much hope in the inventiveness of language, art, and culture, in their ability to hold open the space of the other and to make us reflect not only on our hopes, but also on their limits.[13]

It is essential that students in area studies departments benefit from a similarly multidisciplinary perspective, even if they see themselves

---

[12] Brann, 8-9.

[13] Martin, 'On the Question of Value', 96.

primarily as, say, political scientists. Such multidisciplinary training will render them as versatile thinkers, able to communicate across party lines. This is clearly a valuable skill in virtually any employee, not to mention exactly what the world needs right now, mired as it is in unproductive, hyper-partisan conversations.

Above all, it is essential that students are aware of their own value, and aware of the opportunities created by their expertise in the humanities.[14] Therefore it is incumbent upon lecturers who specialise in pre-modern Arabic literature to impart to their students the full value of what they are learning. Students should be aware that if they conduct a research project and write an essay on a topic pertaining to medieval Arabic literature, they are demonstrating skills that are important to an employer. They are demonstrating the ability to locate and assimilate difficult information, deal sensitively and creatively with the literature of a foreign culture, and express themselves cogently on a complex matter. Recounting such a research project could make extremely engaging anecdotal material to share during a job interview; it would certainly make the student stand out from other candidates. Students should also be aware that understanding the significance of medieval Arabic literature to the development of the world we live in today is valuable in itself; narratives of the past are constantly used to justify or explain current events, and indeed frequent ill-informed references are made to the Crusades, for example, when explaining the bellicose relationship of the West to the East today. An actual knowledge of the medieval Islamic world puts students in a unique position to engage in these global conversations thoughtfully. Teaching Arabic in dialogue with the Classics also usefully serves to blur this false distinction between East and West. A student who not only speaks Arabic and understands politics, but can also think and write about the

---

[14] Opportunity-awareness and self-awareness are the 'O' and the 'S' of the DOTS scheme for helping students improve their employability.

medieval Arabic-speaking world in a well-informed and thoughtful fashion, is indeed a valuable commodity in today's world.

Of course, reading literature in the spirit of open-minded, playful curiosity reveals treasures that such utilitarian approaches will always miss. Approaching a research topic with the question 'how can we best exploit this or manipulate it to our advantage?' is bound to yield shallow and skewed results. So it is to be hoped that while thus priming our students for employment, they will also share with us some of the joys and wonders of Arabic literature, and in swooning at its love poetry, laughing at its wine songs, and marveling at its tales of wonders, will come to understand, viscerally, the humanity they share with the ancient and distant authors that they read, and what truly makes the humanities useful.

References

Brann, Ross. 'An Area Studies Perspective'. In *Do the Humanities Have to Be Useful?*. Ithaca: Cornell University Press, 2006.

'Improving Student Employability: An Ebook for Academics to Help their Students Get Ready to Enter the Labour Market', jobs.ac.uk, accessed June 16, 2017, http://www.jobs.ac.uk/media/pdf/careers/resources/improving-student-employability.pdf.

Jaschik, Scott, 'Millions for 'Strategic' Languages', Jan 4, 2006, https://www.insidehighered.com/news/2006/01/04/language.

Martin, Carolyn. 'On the Question of Value'. In *Do the Humanities Have to Be Useful?*. Ithaca: Cornell University Press, 2006.

Owens, Jonathan. 'The Grammatical Tradition and Arabic Language Teaching: A view From Here'. In *Investigating Arabic: Current Parameters in Analysis and Learning*. Leiden: Brill, 2005.

Ryding, Karin. *Teaching and Learning Arabic as a Foreign Language: A Guide for Teachers*. Washington: Georgetown University Press, 2013.

Savage-Smith, Emilie and Peter Pormann. *Medieval Islamic Medicine*. Washington: Georgetown University Press, 2007.

Scott, Craig. 'What to do with a Degree in Classics'. *The Guardian*, July 24, 2010. https://www.theguardian.com/money/2010/jul/24/classics-degree-graduate-careers.

Stetkevych, Suzanne, 'Observations on Arabic Language Teaching and Learning in the United States: Issues, Challenges, and Ways Forward'. *Arabu Isulami Kenkyu* 11 (March 2013).

Younes, Munther, 'Integrating the Colloquial with Fusha in the Arabic as a Foreign Language Classroom'. In *Handbook for Arabic Language Teaching Professionals in the 21st Century,* edited by Kassem M. Wahba, Zeinab A. Taha, and Liz England. N.J.: Lawrence Erlbaum Associates, 2006.

A Response to Emily Selove

Marjolein Kik & Sanne Rossel

Hello everyone. I am Marjolein Kik, and my name is Sanne Rossel. Thank you, Professor Selove. We both really enjoyed working with your abstract and listening to your talk. Neither of us were familiar with the topic before the start of our research, which illustrates the point you made on the lack of education on the subject.

Professor Selove discussed the influence of the Near East on medieval European culture, a topic often neglected from the discussion of the shaping of European history. We will expand on her talk by concretising her main argument with an example taken from ordinary life. I would like to introduce this example with a quote from a Baghdadi cookbook from the early 14th century: 'The pleasures of this world are six: food, drink, clothing, sex, scent and sound. The most eminent and perfect of these is food, for food is the foundation of the body and the material of life'.[1]

In this paper, we will discuss the influence of the Near East on medieval European cuisine. Some examples of this influence are given in *Food in Medieval Times*: In 711 AD, Arabs from North Africa invaded the Iberian Peninsula – roughly modern-day Andorra, France, Portugal, Spain, and Gibraltar – and brought with them different agricultural methods and foodstuffs such as rice, sugar, and saffron. Around a hundred years later, they invaded Sicily and introduced different foods, like spinach, for example. Three centuries pass. In 1148, sugar was brought back to Europe by crusaders returning from the Holy Land. Richard the Lionheart of England defeated the Saracens under Sultan Saladin and was introduced to the lovely Arabic invention that

---

[1] Schmidt, 'When the West'.

we know as the sorbet.[2]

All of these examples illustrate how Eastern cooking came to Europe through trade, cultural assimilation, and the Islamisation of several countries. This development brought not only the foodstuff itself, but also a renewed respect and appreciation for the culinary arts. The West was now introduced to the indulgent approach to cooking of the East, as high cuisine was an important cultural aspect during the golden age of Baghdad.

As a result of such contact, many different foodstuffs were introduced to Europe, such as citrus fruits, sugar, rice, and different kinds of spices. These spices were of course mainly introduced in the cuisine of the upper class, and they were used for many different purposes.[3]

There is a long-standing myth that spices were sometimes used to cover up the scent of, or camouflage the taste of rotting meat. Now this is of course not the case, because the people who had the money and privilege to buy all of these spices, would not be eating any rotting food, let alone rotting meat.[4] The spices did however serve many other purposes, the most obvious one: adding new flavours to food. Spices were not just added to food, but also to drinks. For example, spices were added to beer to reduce its bitterness, and to create all sorts of new different tastes and kinds of beer. And, as you might know, beer was a very common drink in these times, especially for the upper class.[5] One could not always be sure if water was safe, due to contamination. Beer did not have this problem, due to the production process. It was also lower in alcohol than it is nowadays. So, by the addition of spices, Europe acquired

---

[2] Adamson, *Food in Medieval Times*, 9-11.
[3] Adamson, 9-11.
[4] Schmidt, 'When the West'.
[5] Adamson, 9-11.

a whole new array of beers. It was only because of the spices of the East that they started developing all of these different flavours.[6]

Spices were also believed to have medicinal properties, and were used to heal illnesses or prevent them.[7] They were also used for their scent in perfumes and incense. Finally, they were used in religious ceremonies. Frankincense, for example, was often used in Christian liturgy, as it states in the Bible that this is one of the gifts that Jesus received after his birth.[8]

Especially in the 12th century, there was a reawakening to contact with the East through trade networks, which corresponds to the increase of recipes found after this time period. These texts give us an idea of the way food was preserved and prepared, as well as contemporary dining habits.[9]

It is not just the introduction of new ingredients or the introduction of different methods of cooking, it is also a new appreciation and love for food and culinary culture. Even with their own ingredients and their own methods, the people really started caring about the culinary arts. For example, European cooks started, even in their own recipes, adding sugar or almond milk to create many different types of sauces, stews, porridges, and even pastry fillings. These things had all existed in Europe previously, but after contact was re-established, European cuisines really explored new ways of developing these sauces and pastries to the form in which they are still known today. All of this seems to suggest that the increased contact with the Near East led to a renewed interest in high cuisine in medieval Europe, which was the start of some of Europe's more

---

[6] Holt, *The World of the Crusades*, 322-24.
[7] Freedman, 'Search for Flavors'.
[8] Holt, 322-24.
[9] Schmidt, 'When the West'.

famous cuisines.[10]

As we heard earlier today in Sien's and Artemisia's response to Helle, the senses are quite important to the understanding of different concepts. To illustrate our story, we have prepared a dish that contains a mix of ingredients from different countries. This modern dish consists of dates with orange-infused MonChou and walnuts.

The Near East influenced cuisine in medieval Europe greatly, both with Eastern ingredients and cooking methods, as well as a general appreciation for high cuisine. One of the reasons we chose to expand specifically on the topic of food, is because a love for good food is universal. Today we have, among other things discussed, polarisation and the concept of othering, which at our international university are very prominent topics in the class material of the Western view, the differences between cultures, and so on. These concepts of cultural and social inclusivity and awareness are heavy ones to discuss. Food can be considered very concrete representation of various aspects of culture, social behaviours, and religious or ideological beliefs. It is easier to accept culinary differences between groups, than any of the subjects mentioned above. At the same time, food is where it all starts. To quote our example of an early 14th century Baghdadi cookbook again: 'Food is the foundation of the body and the material of life'.[11] The scholar Paula Arvela describes food to be 'as much of a nutritional and physiological requirement, as it is cultural, symbolic, and meaningful'.[12] So, finding a historical commonality in the cuisines of so many different cultures, might be exactly what we need in order to create more unity.

---

[10] Schmidt, 'When the West'.
[11] Ibid.
[12] Arvela, *Ethnic Food*, 43-56.

References

Adamson, Melitta. *Food in Medieval Times*. Westport: Greenwood Press, 2004.

Arvela, Paula. 'Ethnic Food: The Other in Ourselves'. In *Food: Expressions and Impressions*. Leiden: Brill, 2013.

Freedman, Paul. 'Search for Flavors Influenced Our World'. *Yale University*, March 11, 2003. https://yaleglobal.yale.edu/content/search-flavors-influenced-our-world.

Holt, Andrew, ed. *The World of the Crusades. A Daily Life Encyclopedia* Vol. I, *Arts to Housing and Community*. Santa Barbara: Greenwood, 2019: 322-324.

Ibn al-Ḥasan Ibn al-Karīm, Muhammad. *A Baghdadi Cookery Book*. Translated by Charles Perry. London: Prospect Books, 2005.

Schmidt, Stephen. 'When the West First Tasted the Cuisines of the East'. *Manuscript Cookbooks Survey* (blog), May 2018. https://www.manuscriptcookbookssurvey.org/when-the-west-first-tasted-the-cuisines-of-the-east/.

Reclaiming a Sense of Self in Surreal Times Through Partnership and Creativity

Anna Lee

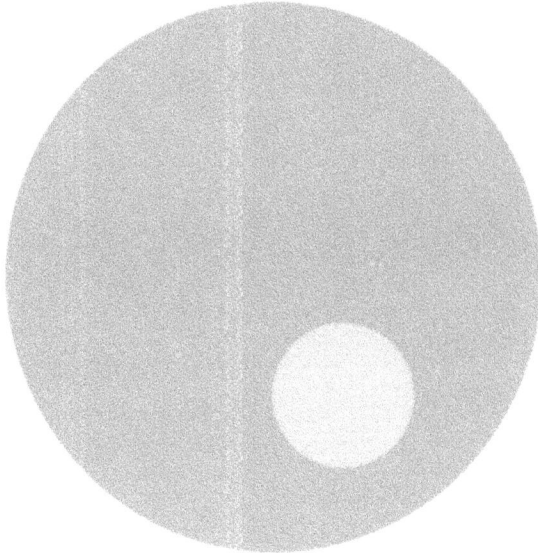

We begin with the self within original community. This is something we cannot control – it is the time, the place, the circumstances we are born into and grow up within. These circumstances impact our view on reality. What is possible, what is not. The world seems like a big place, bigger than us at least.

As we grow and experience more life, we deepen our consciousness and understanding of the world around us. We start to challenge the things that feel restrictive. We may feel like we know all that there is to know. Many people stay in this place. It is familiar. It is self-referential and affirming to the reality we already know.

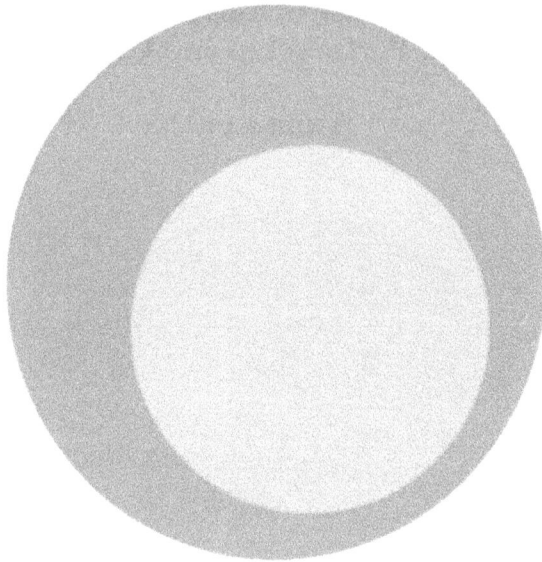

For many of us, it is important to keep learning and asking new questions. Challenge the status quo. We find ourselves growing beyond original community, and that is where things can get scary and lonely. This is where imposter complex may get the better of us. (Hint: You are not alone.) This is also where many people try to 'fake it til you make it', which may create a hollowness to success, as it is built on posturing. The key is to fortify these vulnerable places, not supported by our original cultural structures. We do this by finding mentors, connecting with like-minded friends, sharing with peers in-person or online.

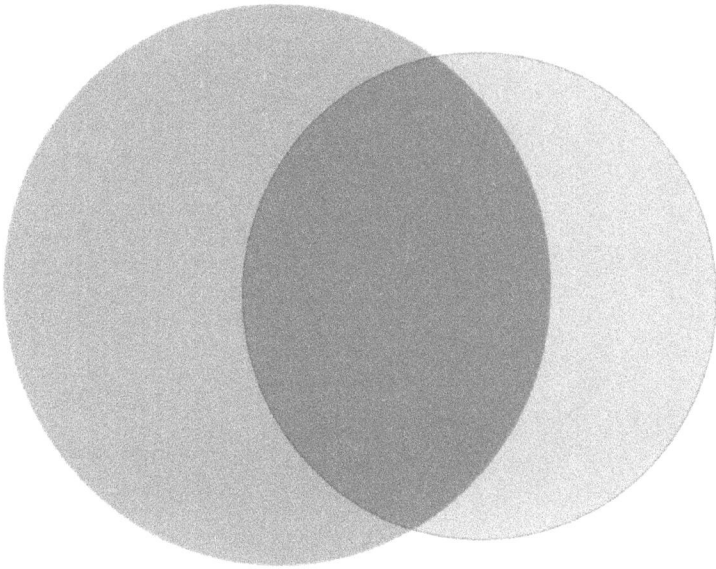

This helps us understand our place in greater community and a broader reality. These places where we feel desperately unseen or unheard, or perhaps a bit lonely, are likely felt by many other people. We struggle to find our place because we have lost our sense of truly belonging within a system that understands, supports, and nurtures us.

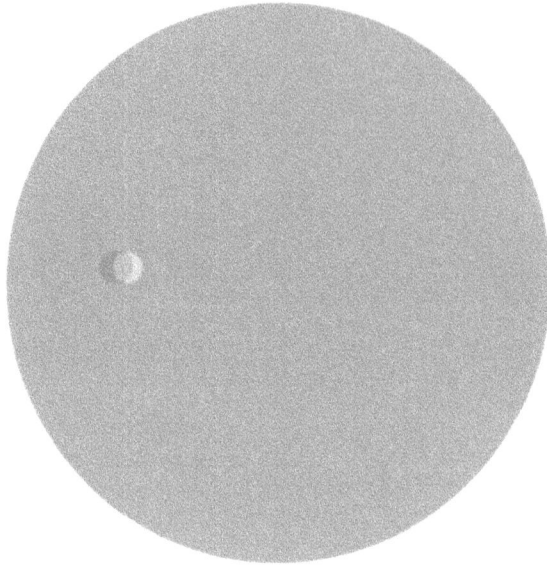

In order to find a greater sense of self in this quickly changing world, we need to differentiate ourselves without disconnecting. We each decide what we will hold on to from our past, our roots, and where we will find new ways of relating. An elegant way of standing in our personal strengths without losing our selves is to be in partnership. This can be with our own creativity, a community, our families and friends. We also let others stand in their own sovereignty.

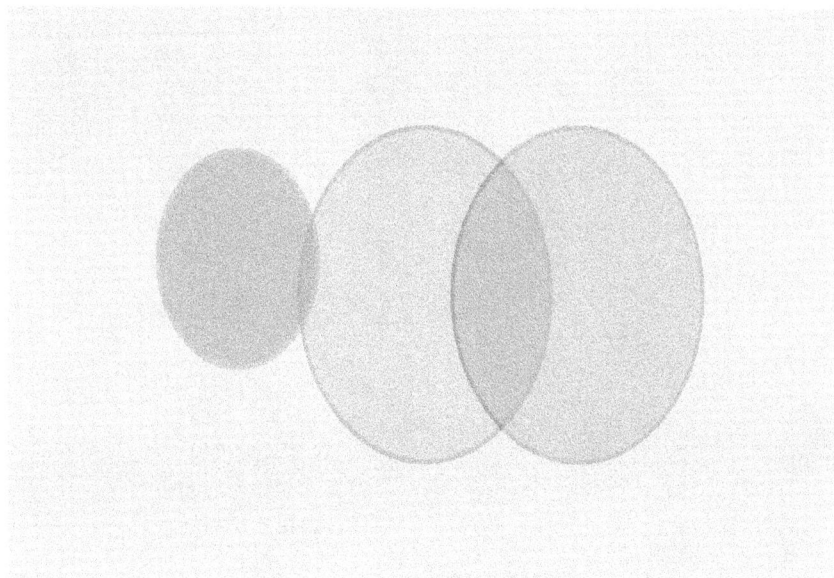

This mode of relating and connecting creates an environment of true collaboration and embodied creativity. We create more together than we could alone, even if we are partnering with our creative self. Even if we are simply having conversations with friends, relating from a place of partnership and honoring the other as well as ourselves, leads to a deeper understanding and connection, where more is possible.

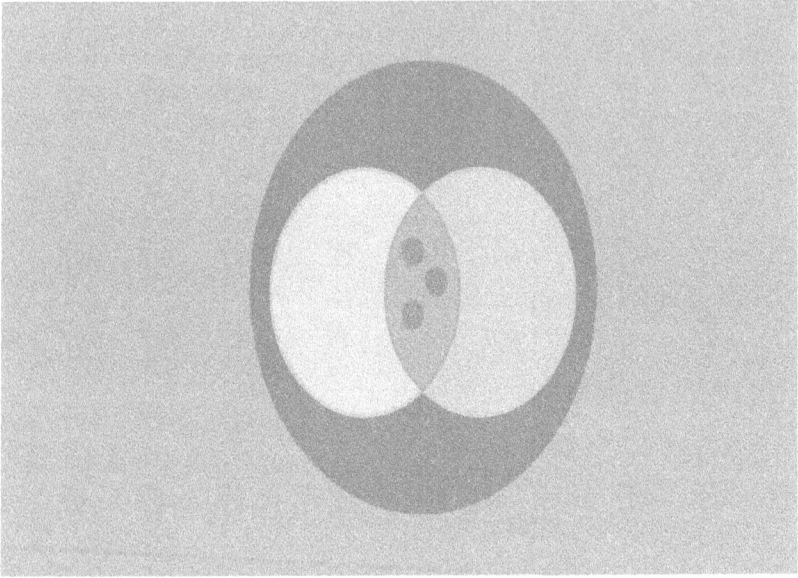

When we experience creating and relating in this deeper way, our work and our lives have a deeper impact. We see greater possibilities and can find solutions to the growing needs of our planet from a more integrated and less ego-centric place.

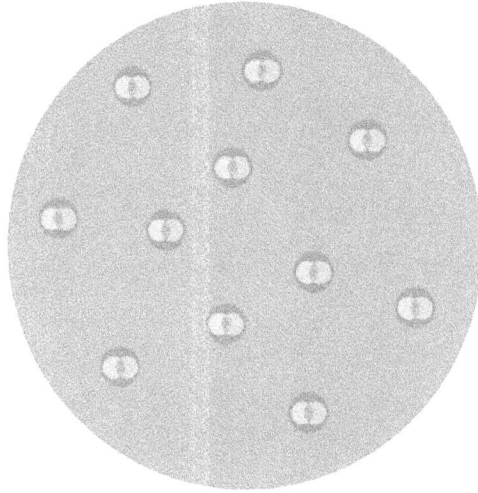

Working from a place of partnership and creativity, we then see ourselves connected to others working in similar ways. Then through many means and technologies, find ourselves connecting immediately and more deeply with those also seeking meaning and solutions.

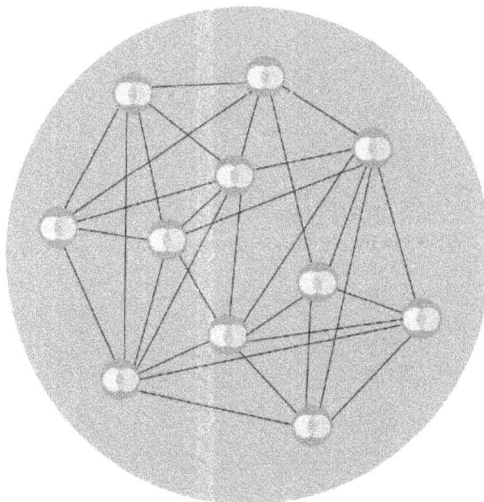

Establishing Heritage in Our Vast Unknown: A Response to Anna Lee

Simone Stals

Just as Anna talked about her own experiences, so will I. Currently, we are looking at a planet that has already been widely explored; we're at a time where we have realized just how large the greater universe is beyond ourselves and people are working on compiling everything they can find and learn in this world to make it accessible. Which is necessary – knowledge should be accessible. But it does mean that the younger members of our societies can interact with everything beyond their immediate community. In my own experience, this means that you can witness growth and expansion beyond your community's limit at a younger age than was possible in the past. And this means you can start to question your place within that community at a younger age.

In my experience, this is terrifying. Having the grandness of the world laid out before you can feel intimidating. And it's difficult not to be overwhelmed by a sense of hopelessness in the face of that. Objects with emotional attachment bring people a sense of comfort when thinking about their tremendous unknown future in the world beyond their own community. This greater community has always done, and will continue to do, things which are completely unrelated to you. This larger reality follows no principles or purpose; it does not care about you. It doesn't care about the location of the Parthenon marbles or making Pepsi pay or that we have the heritage we need to establish and identify ourselves. And it is easy to feel separated from the things you care about in the scope of the great uncaring universe. But we aren't. Since it has no inherent purpose, and life has no inherent purpose, we each get to decide our purpose. We get to decide what it is we care enough about to preserve. Though sometimes it is out of our hands, it is the very fact that we are able to decide what we care about by which caring means something.

And so, heritage, and the value of it, is inherently personal.

Objects which are widely said to represent national heritage are not valued or identified with by all members of that nation. For example, Middelburg is full of well-protected buildings which one could easily argue are heritage, though that does not mean that everyone from here identifies with them. In the entirety of the Netherlands there are almost 62,000 buildings officially considered protected heritage by the Dutch government. The entirety of the country doesn't vote on this of course. But then who decides what should be heritage?

My art history professor introduced a definition of art by American scholar Sylvan Barnet, which stuck with me: 'Art is anything that is said to be art by anyone who ought to know'. This resonated with me because I really like the idea that something is art simply because one feels that it is. Since I've always felt it's the intention behind something that has the power to define it. However, in practice this reveals an institutional theory of art which George Dickie explores referencing the authorized members of the art world who are able to determine something as art. Unfortunately, in reality, this also relates to the esoteric exclusionism of the art world by which certain figures can designate the title of 'art' upon any given piece.

I feel a similar thing is true for heritage. You can't say something is not heritage to someone who feels that it is. By which I mean that you cannot easily convince them otherwise. Of course, the same is true for heritage as it is for the institutional art world; only a chosen few hold the power to officially declare it as such.

When it comes to heritage, we all have the right to be considered 'someone who ought to know'. We all get to say what we feel to be our heritage, meaning that an object gains the title the moment someone says so. Because of this, the reasons one would identify something as their heritage are incredibly broad. Perhaps they are related to someone's family, or represent something to do with their customs. Maybe it represents something a lot more personal to them, like a specific memory, or maybe they see a part of themselves in it. In the same way that any aspect of an object could make it identifiable as heritage, one tiny detail could keep it from being heritage. A simple lack of interaction could make an object not heritage.

Certainly not everyone will feel the same way about a piece of heritage, which is clear when looking at museum discourse. This discourse originates from the fact that museums took roles of preserving heritage upon themselves but can become disconnected from the people and heritage they want to reach and represent. This is especially true for countries whose historical narratives have been influenced by colonizing nations, as the aggression of the colonization creates a lasting dichotomy. The palimpsest of the past traumas are visible in the social organizations which aim to heal what the lucky ones may forget. For example, items are looted from museums in Somalia which the Somalian people have no attachment to, since they do not visit museums.[1] They have no need to visit the museums because the things they consider to be part of their heritage are things like the landscape and their values and traditions. Heritage is something that has to be engaged with in order for it to be heritage.

---

[1] 'Somalia Seeks to Strengthen Management of Its Newly Rehabilitated National Museum', UNESCO World Heritage Centre, https://whc.unesco.org/en/news/2207/.

We give every object its value. We base the value we assign to each specific object on our life experiences. The snake ring I'm wearing now I never take off; my grandfather gave it to me. It represents who I am in his eyes as well as representing my family on a larger scale. Meanwhile, he had found it on the street, polished it up, and upon a whim thought I might like it. And I love it. By this, I want to say that the recognition of value can come from anywhere. Additionally, this can be widespread if we are simply committed to teaching and relaying the held value, just like every student recognizes the value of the phrase 'to be or not to be', they can be taught to see the value of a broad range of heritage. If I were to ask you all what your favourite or most meaningful piece of heritage is, we would come up with widely different answers. Not to mention the fact that we would all interpret the meaning of heritage differently. Since we have the freedom to dedicate ourselves to our interests, we create our own highly personal heritage. So, I believe that heritage *has* to be personal. Every building on the Netherland's protected heritage list is on that list because of the people who cared enough about that specific building to fight for its preservation. Every protected building has an established heritage because of those who cared enough to fight for its preservation. This preservation needs to be enacted though the government of course, but often this need to protect comes from individuals.

The uncaring broad reality is filled with people who care. We each have the ability to find like-minded people who can help support us in our efforts to preserve the objects we love, even though we cannot always see that these people are here and we sometimes forget that we are not alone in the paralyzingly vast unknown. This feeling of isolation leads to the imposter complex, which pulls your own accomplishments into question and makes you fear that you are not enough to be where you are or do what you want to do. The fear that everyone around you knows all the answers and you don't know enough makes creating something new incredibly difficult and stressful. Even though creating isn't always easy, it is always valuable, even if only in an abstract and personal sense. In the grand scheme of things, what you don't know doesn't matter, you can learn. What you don't try, however, that can haunt you. Your mistakes won't be remembered the same way that your accomplishments will. The universe doesn't care if you make what you want to make or preserve what you want to preserve. So do it.

Anselm Kiefer:
Composing in the Asylum of Malignant Memories

Mitchell R. McInnis[∞]

'How is it that the ground itself does not sicken?'

– Walt Whitman

The first time I was in the Netherlands was 1997. I was a young political columnist and journalist eager to discover the realities of tolerant cultures like Amsterdam and Paris. It was the time of politician Wilhelmus Simon Petrus Fortuijn. His politics rigorously engaged many notions I had then about tolerance and inclusivity in the years before and after September 11, 2001, and his assassination disgusted me as few political events ever have. The notion that tolerance is to be defended above open borders was – and remains – controversial. In a world increasingly obsessed with identity politics, individuals like Fortuijn have exerted much effort to redefine masculinity and patrimony. And since the translation of 'heritage' in so many languages carries the nuance and subtext of patrimony, such redefinitions are quite germane to our discussion.

In St. Augustine's *Confessions*, the priest visits the Manichees, an ancient non-Christian religion devoted to the notion that our world is comprised of good and bad particles: atomic-level good and evil.[1] Some of these particles, according to their doctrine, we can control through digestion. For instance, if one eats a fig and expels a belch from that fig, good particles are liberated into the air. In this way, a human agent is able to maximize the quantum of good atoms by merely eating a fig and belching.

It's no more fanciful than devils and angels, surely, though its

---

[1] Aug. *Conf.* 3.10.

symbology is inverted, at least when it comes to figs. It's also an elegant and playful variation on human agency. With equal playfulness, I've wondered over the years whether or not the mathematically inclined Manichees found themselves calculating the number of figs per bad deed. A lie equals three figs, while minor theft equals eight. One imagines the California-sized orchards required to offset the lot of human misdeeds, not to mention collective evils like war.

I thought of the Manichees this week while revisiting the stupefying artistry of Anselm Kiefer's Barjac. No mere canvas or installation, Barjac is a Renaissance town in southern France. Kiefer's town. Kiefer's Barjac is its own commune amidst the series of communes known collectively as Barjac. He bought a roughly 200-acre plot and commenced years ago, creating this art township with only the help of his assistants. Visitors are rare and only upon invitation.

Punctuating the landscape around Kiefer's studio are series of rickety towers reminiscent of medieval Italy, but likewise allusive to a hallucinatory landscape reminiscent of a Dr. Seuss trip. A series of outbuildings and seeming chapels occupy this artscape. Having grown up in Montana, the landscape reminds me of the old state asylum in Warm Springs, a self-contained city-state devoted in equal parts to treating and separating the mentally ill from the population at large. While Kiefer's artistic muses have been described as demonic by some, his city-state is more of an asylum of memory, or a laboratory for the artistic treatment of malignant memories.

As wickedly unique as this landscape is, it is not Kiefer's first Siamese-like twinning of studio and gallery space. In the 1980s, he purchased a brick factory in Buchen, Germany, former site of the extermination camp Buchenwald. In the course of creating monumental canvases and installations, he amassed all manner of leftovers, all of which remain in the transformed factory. Burnt books from a school fire line the wall on one floor, while a small hill of straw in near-adobe state mixed with dirt, sand, paint, and wreckage occupy yet another room on another floor.

Sitting silent and untouched are the factory's brick ovens, suggestive of sinister happenings nearby, and evocative of questions like: What must these brickmakers have been thinking as the smoke from their kiln-baked clay mingled with the curiously acrid smoke from the camp? As the stench from the camp settled over the town? And how many examples of exactly this type of chosen blindness can we indicate in other towns, times, and places outside of Germany?

Inimitable American novelist and activist, James Baldwin, said this of remembering versus forgetting:

> It takes strength to remember, it takes another kind of strength to forget, it takes a hero to do both. People who remember court madness through pain, the pain of the perpetually recurring death of their innocence; people who forget court another kind of madness, the madness of the denial of pain and the hatred of innocence; and the world is mostly divided between madmen who remember and madmen who forget. Heroes are rare.[2]

Returning to Barjac, we see the wreckage and rubble of war carefully curated, bathed in light and seemingly, curiously, growing huge, gray ash-stuffed sunflowers like mushroom caps from scat. In this hothouse of memory, it's difficult not to think of Allen Ginsberg's 'Sunflower Sutra':

---

[2] Baldwin, *Giovanni's Room*, 36.

[....]

'Look at the Sunflower', he said—there was a dead gray shadow against the sky, big as a man, sitting dry on top of a pile of ancient sawdust—

—I rushed up enchanted—it was my first sunflower, memories of Blake—my visions—Harlem

and Hells of the Eastern rivers, bridges clanking Joes Greasy Sandwiches, dead baby carriages, black treadless tires forgotten and unretreaded, the poem of the riverbank, condoms & pots, steel knives, nothing stainless, only the dank muck and the razor-sharp artifacts passing into the past—

and the gray Sunflower poised against the sunset, crackly bleak and dusty with the smut and smog and smoke of olden locomotives in its eye—

[....]

leaves stuck out like arms out of the stem, gestures from the sawdust root, broke pieces of plaster fallen out of the black twigs, a dead fly in its ear,

Unholy battered old thing you were, my sunflower O my soul, I loved you then!

The grime was no man's grime but death and human locomotives,

[....]

and those blear thoughts of death and dusty loveless eyes and ends and withered roots below,

[....]

—all these entangled in your mummied roots—and you there standing before me in the sunset, all your glory in your form!

A perfect beauty of a sunflower! a perfect excellent lovely sunflower existence! a sweet natural eye to the new hip moon, woke up alive and excited grasping in the sunset shadow sunrise golden monthly breeze!

[....]

Poor dead flower? when did you forget you were a flower? when did you look at your skin and decide you were an impotent dirty old locomotive? the ghost of a locomotive? the specter and shade of a once powerful mad American locomotive?

You were never no locomotive, Sunflower, you were a sunflower!

And you Locomotive, you are a locomotive, forget me not!

[....]

—We're not our skin of grime, we're not dread bleak dusty imageless locomotives, we're golden sunflowers inside, blessed by our own seed & hairy naked accomplishment-bodies growing into mad black formal sunflowers in the sunset, spied on by our own eyes under the shadow of the mad locomotive riverbank sunset Frisco hilly tincan evening sitdown vision.[3]

In Kiefer's compositions of saturated sunflowers and war debris, the sunflowers arc from the debris, an upcropping both random and orchestrated, in mid-transformation. And indeed, this transformation is intentional by Kiefer, as he's carefully situated the debris – in this case, two wrecked plane fuselages atop piles of

---

[3] Ginsberg, *Collected Poems*, 146.

near-demolished concrete with rebar dangling mid-air like spiders' legs. He has set these here to grow, to transform, to sublimate into a new form. He gives hint to his task while walking its acreage, commenting how he used to have nightmares, 'but not anymore'.

Has Kiefer, like that fictional, mathematical Manichee, derived an equation for the transformation of the darkest of dark human deeds? An equation for the sublime? Wouldn't this be alchemy? Not that nonsense of turning lead to gold, but the sludge of human evil to mulch that is rained upon, decomposing, and recomposing as mud receptive to gentler seeds blown in from elsewhere, manifesting first as the sooty protuberance of a dying sunflower but eventually as the ecstatic and exuberant sunflower of Van Gogh's visions. That vision is generations away, perhaps, or it may be as close as Barjac. Perhaps.

To get at this notion another way, of the many combatants and refugees I've come to know from my own experiences amidst and following the chaos of lower Manhattan on 9/11, I've often felt my mind and heart's exhaustion surrounding the endless complexity of those events, their causes, and their aftermath. Running through all of them is the agonizing, inexhaustible ache of individual wounds that are never salved by collective politics. These events epitomize our failure as a species to evolve toward the democratic vistas Whitman envisioned. They haunt us with the specters of our own selfishness and lack of true empathy.

To wit, let's visit the work of American philosopher Martha Nussbaum, who has explained the epistemological importance of emotional reactions. In part, this is a function of her mastery of classical texts and the elaborately discussed functions of tragedy among philosophers. If American poetry's move away from confessional poetry to a mix of persona poems and formalism sometimes frustrates a reader's emotional response, it thereby frustrates self-reflection and insight. As Nussbaum writes:

> Our cognitive activity, as we explore the ethical conception embodied in the text, centrally involves emotional response. We discover what we think about these events partly by noticing how we feel; our investigation of our emotional geography is a major part of our search for self-knowledge.[4]

In Sanskrit, it is called *rasa* – literally taste/savor the juice, the essence. Rasa is considered the heart of poetry in the Indian tradition. An emotional response parallel to human experience – and also transcendent of the same – *rasa* is an aesthetic breakthrough both emotional and intellectual. So compelling is this channeling of poetry, Schopenhauer borrowed the notion in his examinations of Indian philosophy, and it became integral to Nietzsche's Dionysian interpretations of classical theater and poetry. Scholar Kathleen Marie Higgins described Nietzsche's interpretation of reader/spectator experience as a 'veritable Dionysian votary, suddenly able to see through the actor to the character, and through the character to the god'.[5]

Federico García Lorca described this essential, dithyrambic fire as the 'Dionysian scream'.[6] Lorca went on with this scorching imagery to help a poet find its sensation in one's veins, 'Seeking the duende there is neither map nor discipline. We only know it burns the blood like powdered glass, that it exhausts, rejects all the sweet geometry we understand'.

[4] Nussbaum, *Fragility*, 15.
[5] Higgins, *Alchemy of Emotion*, 43.
[6] Lorca, *In Search*, 60.

In the end, if we embrace an expiration date on heritage, don't we likewise embrace an expiration date on the collective guilt and shame that come of history's calamities? And is such forgetfulness exculpatory or merely amnesiac?

To draw the question further, I return to Uncle Walt's consummate statement of the same:

I bequeath myself to the dirt to
     grow from the grass I love,

If you want me again look for me
     under your boot-soles.[7]

---

[7] Whitman, *Song of Myself*, Section 52.

References

Augustine. *Confessions, Volume I: Books 1-8*. Translated by Carolyn J.-B. Hammond. Cambridge: Harvard University Press, 2014.

Baldwin, James. *Giovanni's Room*. New York: Dial Press, 1956.

Ginsberg, Allen. *Collected Poems, 1947-1997*. New York: HarperCollins Publishers, 2010.

Higgins, Kathleen Marie. 'An Alchemy of Emotion: Rasa and Aesthetic Breakthroughs'. *The Journal of Aesthetics and Art Criticism* 65, no. 1, (2007): 43-54.

Lorca, Frederico García. *In Search of Duende*. New York: New Directions, 1998.

Nussbaum, Martha. *The Fragility of Goodness: Luck and Ethics in Greek Tragedy and Philosophy*. Cambridge: Cambridge University Press, 2001 [1986, revised edition].

A Response to Mitchell McInnis

Julia Cottrell & Laura du Pree

LP: What Mitchell McInnis has made us consider with his creative and confronting speech is what the impact of humanity's wrongdoings is and how we could deal with it. The malignant memories of those events stay with us. The feeling of guilt they bring forth could be coped with through art, since art can allow us to have such an emotional response that it makes us self-reflect. The poems and even a whole city created by Kiefer are examples of this coping. Keeping this in mind, we would like to get into the last questions posed by McInnis, since these are very important in the process of trying to figure out what place heritage has. We would like to invite you to think about these questions along with us so that we can start up a discussion, so feel free to comment or share thoughts!

JC: The first question that was presented and that we are going to build on is: Is this forgetfulness cleansing, or amnesia? And also, does it matter, considering the impact? Before we open it to everyone, we are going to share our thoughts on these questions.

LP: If this forgetfulness is exculpatory, then it means that people aren't living under the burden of those bad memories anymore, they are free of guilt; but forgetting, as in amnesia, may mean something different, namely that the memories and the guilt coming with it are still there somehow, only repressed. Forgetting is a mechanism to protect oneself against bad human deeds, like McInnis said about 9/11 and its aftermath. It is too big, too complex, too *confronting* a thing to deal with on your own. One can suppress memories or substitute them for better ones and this can be the case for both individuals and whole cultures.[8] Environmental generational

---

[8] Aydin, 'How to Forget the Unforgettable?', 125-37.

amnesia ties in with this. Forgetting could take place because of shifts in generations, which means that in whatever environment one grows up in, this is the environment seen as the norm.[9] So when certain events aren't talked about, they just seem to disappear. We are therefore really wondering if these events are then actually coped with in such a way that there is no guilt and no impact anymore. This is an important question, because suppressing memories could also lead to trauma, which is dangerous since it can disrupt you as an individual and it can also disrupt communities. So, we would like to ask you what your thoughts are on this question:

Is forgetting cleansing or is it amnesia?

MK: I also think that really depends on what the purpose behind [the forgetting] is. Are you forgetting it on purpose? Are you making yourself or others forget things on purpose because you don't want to think about it, or is it unconscious? Because I think if you are consciously trying to forget something, like if you're consciously erasing things from history, or suppressing someone's voice, that's very different than if you are trying to forget something to protect yourself because it is too much to deal with and it's disrupting your life. I think both can be the case, but it's important to identify which it is. And it can also, I guess, be both sometimes.

AL: I think that by saying it's either forgetting or it's cleansing makes it too simple, I guess. It's something in between that is the place we should really be interested in. I visited – a couple of weeks ago – the National History Museum in Washington with a group of people, and by the end of the visit about half of us were crying at some point or another. Was that cleansing? I don't know if that was cleansing. But there was a realisation – actually, most of us know – but there was a *confrontation*. And

---

[9] Kahn, 'Human Relation', 41; and Koleva, 'Daughters' Stories', 202.

there was the question of what does this mean? So you leave the place in confusion. You know that there's guilt involved; you don't know whether it's your guilt, or where you can put the guilt. This confusion and this new realization that this matters: That is essential to an aesthetic experience, that it leaves you in a way to wonder. So it's neither total cleansing or forgetting that interests us, but what is there in between, but it's a very good question.

DG: Yes, I was also thinking about this. I'm not sure if this is a binary that speaks to all sorts of experiences. What if it becomes something different? I was thinking about colonialism as an example of this, because that's what I'm most familiar with. I tend to think of myself as a product of colonialism, because my mother is from Sri Lanka and my father is from America. So how can that become something completely different? How am I not bound up in that guilt in a way but still am? I don't know. I don't have any answer, but how [does that fit into that binary]?

SR: Something that I always kind of struggle with is the idea of collective guilt, or guilt from ancestry or inheritance. For example, I am fully Dutch, and I know we have a really bad history with colonization especially with the Dutch East Indies, and I know that not acknowledging that would make me feel that I'm guilty. But what I find difficult is that once I acknowledge the guilt of my ancestors, am I then relieved of that guilt or do I have to keep doing something with that? Because in a way, if I acknowledge it, and then not further act on it, does that mean I have forgotten or am I then released of my guilt? I don't know how I even have to look at that sort of thing, because I feel there's not a single thing I'd be able to do in such a situation that would not be either bad or me carrying a guilt that I don't believe is fair for me to carry as a person.

BN: This is super interesting what you just talked about in the context of you acknowledging the guilt and then what next, but its super important, maybe, to also realise that this history has also maybe inhibited your tendencies or things that you [would have done]. And if you come from a culture where there was a genocide, of course in this culture there are going to be red flags and other things that are inherited generation after generation and for you to, like, acknowledge this guilt that you feel of your own parents. There has not only been guilt in the way of 'oh yeah now I need to be punished or something', but also maybe to realise the tendencies that may be inherited from past generations.

LM: May I build on this really quickly? [To Anna Lee, also wanting to speak.] I'm so sorry, otherwise I would have to start this conversation over. [To speakers] I don't think you expected this to be like this, so thank you. You know I was thinking that acknowledging the guilt and not feeling bad about something you did not cause, it's something that I've actually been exploring. So many things have been talked about that speak to me directly as somebody who has been a victim of colonialism, but also now, finding myself participating in the colonization of America as someone who is married to a family that came to Minnesota from Norway in the 1800s and benefitted from the Homestead Act. I realised how heavy I am in my privilege, living on stolen land. And what do I do with that? So going further, you know, further than the guilt, is like making sure I can [move on]. Maybe the heritage can be transmitted to the next generation, but not as a 'I deserve to have this land' in my village, because of how that happened. I was very shocked when I was talking to my husband to find out he does not even know exactly how his family came, when they came. And he is an intelligent man. So I'm thinking about this guy, who is an author, and who is not even interested in finding 'how did we end up here?', 'how did we have this land?'. So I want to make sure that the narrative [is preserved]. And so my responsibility is in the stories, and really making sure I amplify the Native American connection to the land that I inherited. Basically, doing something positive out of something I could not control.

AL: Absolutely. I think that's so beautiful. The only thing I'll add is that the impact of privilege and the impact of trauma are two very different things and I think the body holds that differently. We have expectations, when we have not experienced trauma that the colonized have experienced. They have trauma in their body, and the colonizers – if I could just make it black and white – only experience privilege. And so generations later, it's really hard to understand because we don't feel it in the same way, our privilege, because we have just accepted it. Trauma feels more like trying to get over it. That's also an acceptance. And so when you feel like: When do we deal with the pain of our ancestors? There are different leading modalities. What needs to happen in both is different.

References

Aydin, Ciano. 'How to Forget the Unforgettable? On Collective Trauma, Cultural Identity, and Mnemotechnologies'. *Identity* 17, no. 3 (2017): 125-37.

Kahn, Peter H., Rachel L. Severson, Jolina H. Ruckert. 'The Human Relation With Nature and Technological Nature'. *Current Directions in Psychological Science* 18, no. 1 (2009): 37-42.

Koleva, Daniela. 'Daughters' Stories: Family Memory and Generational Amnesia'. *The Oral History Review* 36, no. 2 (2009): 188-206.

Heritage, Conflict, and the Media in Contemporary Burundi

Laetitia Mizero Hellerud

General Background

Burundi is a small landlocked country located in what is known as the Great Lakes region in eastern Africa. The landscape is varied and beautiful. Burundi has a mean elevation of 1,504 m above sea level. It has an equatorial climate where rainfall varies by altitude, although the climate generally is moderate. Its terrain is hilly and mountainous with some plateaus.

Burundi is 10,746 square kms (27,834 square miles) and has a dense, mostly agro-pastoral population of 10.86 million (2017). For the sake of comparison, the Netherlands sit on 16,039 square kms (41,543 square miles) with a population of 17.16 million (2017). There are three ethnic groups in Burundi. However, the notion of 'ethnic group' or 'tribe' as applied to Burundi has, at times, generated some controversies and debates among historians and anthropologists. Unlike other countries with tribes and ethnic groups, which can easily and clearly be distinguished by language, customs or traditions, territory, and other differentiating criteria, Burundian people defy this interpretation.

Wikipedia defines ethnic group or ethnicity as 'a category of people who identify with each other, usually on the basis of presumed similarities such as common language, ancestry, history, society, culture, nation, or social treatment within their residing area'.[1] In his attempt to explain the concept of ethnicity as either 'invented, imagined, or mythologized', René Lemarchand, a renowned

---

[1] https://en.wikipedia.org/wiki/Ethnic_group.

historian and professor at the University of Pennsylvania writes in his book, *The Dynamics of Violence in Central Africa*:

> Ethnicity is never what it seems. What some see as ancestral atavism, others see as a typically modern phenomenon, anchored in colonial rule. Where neo-Marxists detect class interests parading in traditional garb, mainstream scholars unveil imagined communities. And whereas many see ethnicity as the bane of the African continent, other think that it could provide the basis for a moral social contract and that it contains within itself the seeds of openness and accountability.[2]

The three ethnic groups of Burundi are: the *Hutu* (Bantu) representing the majority at 85% of the population, followed by the *Tutsi* (Hamitic) at 14%, and a small percentage of *Twa* (Pygmy) or 1% of the population. These populations are believed to have lived in Burundi for at least 500 years. For more than 200 of those years, Burundi was an independent kingdom where the Hutus and Tutsis lived with known tensions. Relative to the geopolitical context of the cyclical conflicts in the Great Lakes region of Africa, Professor Lemarchand remarks:

> In its efforts to make more 'legible', the complex ethnic configurations of the region, the colonial state contributed significantly to formalizing and legitimizing the Hutu-Tutsi polarity.[3]

Historically and even today, the Twas have been ignored, at best, and oppressed, at worse, by the other two groups.

---

[2] Lemarchand, *Dynamic of Violence*, 49.
[3] Lemarchand, 9.

In 1858 the British explorers Richard Burton and John Hanning Speke were the first Europeans to visit Burundi and in 1890, the Kingdoms of Urundi (Burundi) and Ruanda (Rwanda) became part of German East African colonies.

After the First World War and Germany's defeat, it surrendered the territory to Belgium through a mandate by the League of Nations. Both colonizing countries ruled Burundi and Rwanda as a European colony known as Ruanda-Urundi until 1962, when Burundi and Rwanda each respectively gained their independences, on July 1st.

There are not many written documents about Burundi's pre-colonial era, other than notes and diaries from early explorers and Catholic missionaries who brought Christianity to Burundi and other colonized countries in Africa. Long before print, Burundians had a rich oral tradition which helped to not only preserve and transmit historical accounts, generation after generation, but also assisted elders in educating the young about important life lessons. Although Burundi has three official languages (Kirundi, French, and English), Kirundi is recognized as the sole national language.

The Nature of Conflicts in Burundi

Research by different scholars concluded that the Twas (artisans, hunter-gatherers) are the original indigenous people in Burundi. The (Bantu) Hutus settled in the area in the 1300s, followed by the (Hamitic) Tutsis in the 1400s. Burundi has a patriarchal system where one inherits their father's ethnic group. Unlike other African countries with ethnic groups and tribes, this is a sensitive topic that is not openly talked about or discussed in Burundi. The only time Burundians had ethnic affiliation mentioned on any official document was in 1933 (initiated by Belgian colonizers) and perhaps for some years afterwards.

Tensions between these ethnic groups have become violent on several occasions since independence. The International Commission of Inquiry for Burundi presented by the United Nations Security Council in 1996 described two instances of violence as genocides, namely the 1972 mass killings of Hutus by a Tutsi-dominated army, and the 1993 mass killings of Tutsi by the majority Hutu populace.[4] Recently, more than 4,000 mass graves have been identified in Burundi and ABC News has reported that six of the largest graves opened by Burundian authorities contained more than 6,000 bodies.

In a segment on deconstructing social identities as pertaining to Burundi, Rwanda, and the Democratic Republic of the Congo, Professor Lemarchand states:

> Tempting as it is to view ethnic diversity as the central determinant of violent behavior in the region, the evidence shows otherwise. To the extent that it does provide a meaningful point of reference, ethnicity is not a throwback to primeval enmities. Whether socially constructed, manipulated, invented, or mobilized, it is a recent phenomenon, even when its roots are sometimes traceable to precolonial times (as in the case of Banyamulenge). Its contours, moreover, are constantly shifting, as are the human targets against which it is directed. Communities seen as allies one day are viewed as enemies the next. New coalitions are built for short-term advantage, only to dissolve into warring factions when new options suddenly emerge. In this highly fluid political field, conflict is not reducible to any single identity marker.

---

[4] United Nations, International Commission of Inquiry for Burundi, Final Report by the United States Institute of Peace, S/1996/682.

It's better conceptualized as involving different social boundaries, activated at different points in time, in response to changing political stakes.[5]

Lemarchand's analysis sums up the nature of the cycles of violence in Burundi and the Great Lakes region in general. Although the conflicts in Burundi have been consistently and simplistically labelled as ethnically based, each round could be 'separately diagnosed in connection with complex variables specific to or aggravated by the circumstances of the time it occurs'.

The Role of Social Media

Prior to the 1990s, the media in Burundi were government owned. There were daily newspapers and periodicals (Ubumwe, Ndongozi, Le Renouveau du Burundi), and radio and television (Radiodiffusion et Télévision Nationales du Burundi, RTNB) which published and broadcasted government-endorsed views. For a long time, radio has been the main source of information in this country where the majority of the population cannot afford to buy a television. The illiteracy rate and poverty level are both high enough to make newspapers inaccessible to many. Overall, the news was monitored and scrutinized by the reporters and their respective media networks to always put the government in a good light. Government officials were typically not contradicted or questioned, and the information broadcasted was seldom fact-checked. Not operating within those parameters had severe consequences including losing one's job and even being jailed. The fear of contradicting people in power was widespread among the population who suspected fellow citizens of spying on behalf of the government. People were so guarded that they would not even make verbal jokes amongst friends about the president or anyone

---

[5] Lemarchand, 7.

within his administration. My father, as well as the person who would later be the first democratically elected president of Burundi, Melchior Ndadaye, (these two individuals also happened to be neighbors and acquaintances) were jailed in 1990 after denouncing – in a public meeting with Governor J.B. Basomingera of Gitega – what they thought were flagrant examples of abuse of power by the government. A search for reported or archived references of this incident was inconclusive, perhaps because the occurrence was not isolated or because it was not a 'positive' accomplishment by the so-called political 'leadership'. As a disclaimer and to give more weight to the recollection of this incident, my father (Pierre-Claver Sendegeya) was one of the three presidential candidates in those democratic elections of June 1, 1993.

In a referendum that approved a new constitution in 1992, multiple political parties were officially founded or allowed to work in the open in preparation for the 1993 elections. Many forms of independent media were also created for the first time and covered different perspectives, often opposing the opinions of members of the dominant party in power and the government itself. Typical to authoritarian regimes and newly established 'democracies', the level of media censorship (both self-imposed and government-enforced) was more than palpable. Over the years, many privately owned radios like Radio Isanganiro, Bonesha FM, and African Public Radio (RPA) were broadcasting in Kirundi, French, English, and Swahili. Beyond the state owned RTNB, other private television channels were also launched in multiple languages (e.g. Heritage TV, Télé Renaissance). Some international radio stations like the Voice of America (VOA), Radio France Internationale (RFI), and the British Broadcasting Company (BBC) do have a limited reception radius in some cities in Burundi. The internet did not become widely used or supported until early 2000 when the government, as well as some foreign aid groups, invested in quality connectivity towers.

Although there is no law prohibiting freedom of expression per se, working in the media industry in Burundi soon turned out to be dangerous. The Committee to Protect Journalists (CPJ), a nonprofit organization that promotes press freedom worldwide has documented attacks on journalists in Burundi since 1992.[6] When President Nkurunziza was contemplating a controversial and contested third term in 2015, journalists from local major independent media who reported the frequent protests among the population and the loud uproar by political opposition parties were persecuted, killed, and forced to leave the country in search of safety. Their media companies' headquarters were either closed or burned down. Some of their material was confiscated.

Many of these journalists who were able to escape continued their work reporting on the human rights violations and shedding light on the level of violence in the country they fled. They were able to do so thanks to their respective companies' online tools or presence from foreign countries where they had relocated. Using different websites, Facebook pages, Twitter, and Instagram, they continued denouncing the atrocities of the Burundian regime as well as sharing other newsworthy stories. WhatsApp is another platform consistently used to distribute news articles, video recordings, and more, especially among specific groups of Burundians in the diaspora.

These digital media resources do help in providing different accounts or perspectives of the situation in the country compared to the partisan, government-endorsed information broadcasted by the national radio, television, or published in state-owned newspapers. Human rights groups and peace advocacy organizations working in Burundi use social media to disseminate some of their messages. Facebook pages like Ndondeza (translated in English as 'Help me

---

[6] www.cpj.org.

find') and other similar online outlets do play a significant role in the search for victims of kidnapping, a disturbingly frequent occurrence. Although the kidnapped victims are seldomly found alive, if found at all, at least the online followers or consumers interested in the happenings in Burundi become aware of the pervasive nature of this type of human rights violation. In the absence of these resources, it is fair to assume that only the people who are close to the victim would know of their disappearance, illegal imprisonment, torture, murder, etc.

The availability, relatively affordable cost, and immediacy of social media can be an advantage to quality information access when professional journalists or organizations utilize them to benefit the consumers or followers. However, one of the many downsides is that there is a significant number of inaccurate, incomplete, or unverified pieces of information, images, or videos circulating quickly and creating all kinds of reactions. In the case of Burundi, this type of false news negatively impacts the already complicated overall political climate and fuels the ongoing violence between whichever factions are fighting. The type of information shared through social media oftentimes lack objectivity, balance, accuracy, and professionalism, especially when initiated by untrained people, which is what happens in most of the cases. More and more people own a cellular phone, even in Burundi, a country that is ranked as the third poorest country in the world based on the Gross Domestic Product (GDP) per capita.[7]

An article excerpt from the Research and Action for Peace website, states:

Social media has a major impact on how we

---

[7] 2019 World Population Review, https://worldpopulationreview.com.

communicate, interact, and understand the world. It is now intricately linked with global, national, and local politics. We take this for granted. But we are now coming to understand that social media is used in particular ways in societies experiencing ongoing violent conflict or emerging from a period of war. For those of us who analyze complex conflicts and their resolution, understanding how social media promotes conflict – and peace – is critical and becoming more so with each day.[8]

Conclusion

Technology is continuously shaping lives and impacting the direction the world goes. The use of media in provoking and fueling conflicts is something that has been used throughout history. One can go back to Hitler's Germany and look at the use of newspaper, the radio, and even television to spread anti-Jewish propaganda. One can also fast forward to 1994 and go to Rwanda, the country directly north of Burundi with the same population makeup and similar distressing cycles of internal conflicts often leading to violence. Traditional media was used to spread anti-Tutsi propaganda that objectified this group and created an atmosphere which contributed to the systematic killing of between 800,000 to a million (depending on the source of information) Tutsis and 'moderate' Hutus in four months. It had been widely documented that the radio was largely used to relay messages to the populace.

> During the 1994 Rwandan Genocide, radio broadcasts played an important role in inciting ordinary citizens to take part in the massacres of

---

[8] Branka Marijan, 'Social media and conflict', *Ploughshares Monitor* 39, no. 4 (2018).

their Tutsi, and moderate Hutu, neighbours. Two major radio stations transmitted hate propaganda to the illiterate masses – Radio Rwanda, and Radio Télévision des Milles Collines (RTLM).[9]

The same media used to destroy and kill can certainly also be used to build peace. But none of this is new. What is new and troubling is the fact that social media is readily available to many and instantaneous, giving it the potential to reach the maximum of people in no time. It behooves humanity to exercise a great deal of accountability when applying technology, both individually and as a collective. People need to pause, think, research, discuss, and network with regards to individuals' roles in these issues, but also the responsibility of the different relevant systems, including the international community. Reflecting on all these issues begs the following moral questions:

What kind of social media information consumer does one want to be?

How does one use the information they receive and for what purpose?

How do the actions of spreading a particular piece of information align with one's value system or moral compass?

And hopefully this last note to self is also a remark that might resonate with many readers: Commit to lifelong learning as technology is ever changing.

---

[9] www.concordia.ca/research/migs/resources/rwanda-radio-transcripts.html.

References

Chrétien, Jean-Pierre and Jean-Francois Dupaquier. *BURUNDI 1972, Au Bord des Génocides*. Paris: Karthala Editions, 2007.

Kaneza, Eloge Willy. 'Largest Mass Graves Uncovered in Burundi with 6,000 Bodies'. *ABC News*, February 17, 2020. https://abcnews.go.com/ International/wireStory/largest-mass-graves-uncovered-burundi-6000-bodies-69028787.

Lemarchand, René. *The Dynamic of Violence in Central Africa*. Philadelphia: University of Pennsylvania Press, 2009.

Marijan, Branka. 'Social Media and Conflict'. Ploughshares Monitor 39, no. 4 (2018).

A Response to Laetitia Mizero Hellerud

Daantje van de Linde

First of all, I would like to thank Laetitia for giving an exciting lecture, and everyone else for joining the conference today. My name is Daantje and I will talk you through my response to Laetitia's presentation. My focus will be on the prevention of conflict and the realization of peace through the use of social media, as a response to the question of whether we should be worried about the abundant use of it. In doing so, I will focus on the radio as an effective medium to prevent conflict, followed by an example of a study done in Burundi to investigate how we can employ social media to find ourselves at the advantage.

In 2016, a study was published by R. Bilali, J. Vollhardt, and J. Rarick concerning the media in Burundi. They used radio dramas to see what impact it had on listeners, regarding violence and positive relations, and compared this to the behaviour of non-listeners. Radio La Benevolencija broadcasted the radio drama *Murikira Ukuri (Shedding Light on the Truth)* in Burundi, reaching a listener rate of approximately 65%. It is about 'a conflict between two fictional ethnic groups that differ in educational level and income opportunities . . . making the story very accessible to Burundians, who can relate to the complex power relations and grievances of the fictional groups'.[1] They tried to find ways in which such dramas might influence people's attitudes towards ethnic conflicts and violence.

The theory they worked with contains the following five points:

---

[1] Bilali, Vollhardt, and Rarick, 'Assessing the Impact', 222.

1. Listeners reach an understanding of the origins of violence, which is automatically a contribution to its prevention and might even lead to active bystandership;

2. Listeners will communicate new social norms;

3. Because the stories are fictional, listeners are able to learn about different opinions in a non-threatening way;

4. Some dramas are about two villages cooperating, causing the listeners to create the image of positive intergroup interactions;

5. The dramas portray both positive and negative character of both sides of the conflict. This makes the listeners think critically of concepts like 'good versus evil' and 'us versus them'.

The results of the study were interesting. The radio drama had a positive effect on several aspects, such as tolerance towards other people, intergroup trust, social distance, competitive victimhood, and in-group superiority.[2]

Could social media be used in this same way? Could we use Facebook, Twitter, Instagram, and other platforms in the same way the radio was used to broadcast the radio dramas? I am convinced we can. In fact, it might be as simple as just putting videos online of people telling such stories. These can be made into podcasts, which can then be put online. Perhaps it does seem a bit too simple this way. I agree, but some of the negative aspects of social media – being readily available to many people or allowing people to spread

---

[2] Bilali, Vollhardt, and Rarick, 229.

false news more easily – can be turned into positive ones in this case. Where most people would have had a radio a couple of years ago, they now have phones with access to social media. If we can find a way in which radio dramas like these can be transmitted through social media instead of a radio, it might be possible to achieve similar effects. So, perhaps we should not fear the harm that social media can cause, but should embrace them and use them to our advantage, to improve social relations and prevent future conflicts.

As Vladimir Bratic mentions in his article, 'Examining Peace-Oriented Media in Areas of Violent Conflict', there are three types of violence: direct violence, structural violence, and cultural violence. Cultural violence is an invisible form of violence and occurs often in the symbolic sphere of action.[3] For example: symbols, flags, and speeches, but also texts or images produced by (social) media. The point I am trying to make here is described clearly in his article:

> Artefacts of cultural violence have been perceived as powerful tools that not only incite conflict but also disseminate discrimination. It is within this theoretical framework of cultural violence that the influence of media on both conflict and peace gains a prominent role. Within the domain of cultural violence, media become a venue that can give life to the artefacts of conflict and the ideas for peace.[4]

The argument is that media intervention, when it is peace-oriented, can eliminate negative effects of cultural violence. This means that social media can be used this way too.

Perhaps, there need to be certain criteria in order to have social

---

[3] Bratic, 'Examining', 492.
[4] Bratic, 492.

151

media work in a positive way. These could be something along the lines of having a certain purpose while creating content, instead of just reporting what is happening. Or having an organisation behind creating that content, so it has a clear structure and is more useful in getting the message across. One must be cautious, however, when institutionalising social media, as the strength of social media should not belong to a distinct group but be accessible to all people, allowing everyone to share personal views and experiences instead of bringing across filtered messages. Of course, you will always have to deal with the ways social media can be abused, but we have to find ways in which we can use social media to the benefit of people and to be able to use its positive aspects to fight the negative ones. Social media can, for example, be employed as a means to combat false or negative information by creating counter or alternative narratives; they could allow people to show what is happening in their lives, to portray a genuine image of what is going on in a particular area or during a particular conflict; or they can create the opportunity for different social groups to meet and connect – whether you belong to the same party or not. And this is only a gist of the endless list of possibilities.

So, should we be worried about the abundant use of social media? Perhaps, but in my opinion that is only the case if we fail to utilize them as a way of preventing conflict and realizing peace to resist cultural violence. The radio dramas in Burundi have proved effective and I am convinced we can adopt this framework and project it onto social media channels to achieve similar results. While it goes beyond the scope of this talk, it would be interesting to further investigate recent studies on social media and their workings, and the role of institutions and organisations in this.

References

Bilali, Rezarta, Johanna Ray Vollhardt, and Jason Ray David Rarick. 'Assessing the Impact of a Media-based Intervention to Prevent Intergroup Violence and Promote Positive Intergroup Relations in Burundi'. *Journal of Community & Applied Social Psychology* 26, no. 3 (2016): 221-235.

Bratic, Vladimir. 'Examining Peace-Oriented Media in Areas of Violent Conflict', *International Communication* 70, no. 6 (2008): 487-503.

Un/Seen Histories: Native News

Nancy Mykoff

About four years ago I got my hands on a Native American newspaper called the *Teton Times*.[1] It is published weekly on the Standing Rock Reservation in North Dakota. The subtitle, 'Pride in our Past, Faith in our Future', intrigued me. So, I turned the pages of the newspaper. As I did, stories and histories began to unfold. Articles and editorials titled, 'Healing Your Trauma', and 'Invisible No More', transfixed and educated me.

I learned, for instance, that July is 'awareness month'. It is 'the month to comfort parents who have lost children'. This sentence struck me as odd. Didn't they mean children that had lost their parents? I re-read the sentence a few times. And then, I read on. The article continued: 'Although every July is acknowledged as a national month of awareness, the majority of our indigenous people work hard to comfort their grieving relatives all year round'.[2] I would come to learn that grief was, and is, a central part of Indian life.

I looked for insight into the year-round grieving in the *Spirit World* section of the *Teton Times*. It features obituaries that I will refer to as 'death narratives', because they read like biographies. The sense of movement, or of moving on, strikes me. The youth of those that died takes my breath away. I read, for example, about Torri His Chase.

---

[1] Articles and editorials alternatively refer to Native Americans as Native Americans, indigenous people, the People, and Indians. For example, an editorial in *Native Sun News Today*, concludes that, 'Indian is who and what we are'. It argues, '...we don't say 'Cowboys and Indigenous', or 'Cowboys and Natives'....No, it is 'Cowboys and Indians', That what we played as kids...The word Native', it concludes, 'was picked by a bunch of white newspaper editors trying to find a way to describe us Indians in a way that we would not find offensive'.

[2] 'Honoring the Memory', *Teton Times* 17, no. 33, (July 30 -July 10), 4.

She died when she was twenty-five years old and was 'daddy's girl' when she lived. Torri 'loved lying in front of the TV watching Lifetime for hours, and eating popcorn with all her sisters'.[3]

I also learned about Anthony Nathen Guy Iron Moccasin. He died when he was twenty-two, and was a runner when he was alive. He also, 'enjoyed walking, skateboarding, drawing, playing his guitar, hanging out with friends, and video games'.[4] As I continued reading, I came to know Anthony and found myself grieving with his parents.

I also read about eighty-three year old Aurelia Irene Marks who, 'After her children were gone from home, raised her grandson Winston and granddaughter TeraJo. She enjoyed making Indian dance costumes as well as . . . going to church gatherings and gospel music'.[5] Her life, like those of other 'older' people that had died, told me something about family, religion, struggles, and joy in Indian Country.

But it was the deaths of the young that haunted me. The average age was forty. My question was why? What happened in the past, and what was happening in the present, that resulted in the deaths? When I could not find insights, or even acknowledgement, in my American history textbooks or favorite news outlets, I decided to explore the local and national indigenous newspapers that are at the center of this research project. The former is online and the latter in hard copy. Both speak to the presence of the past. One bleeds into the other. Together they present 'different' pasts unseen by 'American' society.

The Indian past that is seen in 'American' textbooks spotlights

[3] 'Spirit World', *Teton Times* 7, no. 11, (Jan. 30-Feb. 6), 9.
[4] 'Spirit World', *Teton Times* 17, no. 1 (Nov. 21-Nov. 28), 6.
[5] 'Spirit World', *Teton Times* 7, no.11, (Jan. 30-Feb. 6), 9.

contact, conquest, relocation, and the 'Indian Wars'. First, European colonists meet Indian inhabitants. Next, Indians die off from disease, like small pox, that decimate whole tribes. Those that survive make it into the chapter devoted to Jacksonian America (1830s), where Indians are removed from their homelands on to uninhabitable lands set aside by the U.S. government and called reservations. They are ushered from one to the other by the U.S. Army. The most familiar of these journeys is the Cherokee 'Trail of Tears', when the Cherokee tribe was forced to relocate west of the Mississippi when gold was discovered on their homeland in Georgia. Approximately 16,000 people walked the 5,000 miles to 'Indian Country'. Approximately 4,000 died before they arrived.

The next chapter to feature Indians is usually titled 'The West'. It tells about the 'Indian Wars' fought against the Indian people so that European settlers could claim Indian land for their homes. The 'Wars' are won at the battle called Wounded Knee in 1890, where unarmed people were shot to death for performing a dance called the Ghost Dance. Whilst the textbook renditions don't celebrate the 'battle', they also don't elaborate on the massacre or its continuing consequences.

Both the massacre and its consequences are voiced in Indian culture. For example, a recent article titled, 'Removing the Stain of Wounded Knee', notes that, 'according to officers present at the shooting, the soldiers were greatly excited, surrounding the Lakota and shooting wildly without aiming their guns. Warriors, squaws, children, ponies, and dogs . . . went down before that un-aimed fire. The soldiers also killed or wounded dozens of their own comrades positioned across the surrounding circle'.[6] Wounded Knee signaled the vanishing of Native Americans from white sight.

---

[6] "Removing the Stain of Wounded Knee' Bill introduced', *Teton Times* 17, no. 33 (July 3-July 10), 2.

It was documented in images like *The Vanishing Indian* by Edward Curtis.

Native Americans do, however, appear in photographs throughout the twentieth century. They are positioned as supporting characters in a rather heroic national narrative, where American 'good' battles the evil 'other'. An example is the image of U.S. Marines raising the American flag over Mount Suribachi, Iwo Jima in February 1945. Ira Hayes, a Pima Indian, is one of the soldiers pictured in the photograph.

Missing from the historical pictures are the children and adults with unique stories and shared burdens. Missing also is the impact of 'lateral trauma' which, according to the *Teton Times* is, '...when people who are victims of dominance turn on each other rather than confront the system oppressing them'. The enduring pain of Wounded Knee and the violent crimes that kill across Indian country today, are blamed on, ' . . . trauma carried at the cellular level to do the suffering of our ancestors'.[7] Thus, the deaths of today are traced to the murders of yesterday.

A letter to the editor, written on behalf of a teenaged girl that killed herself, speaks to the suffering from lateral trauma and 'Indian invisibility'. Titled 'I am a Lakota Teen', it begins, 'I am a Lakota teen. I live in the shadows of America, within its prisoner of war camps now called reservations. Have you seen me? Do you know that I exist? I have survived countless nights of my earlier childhood when I went to bed hungry, when I was molested, when I was beaten, when I shivered from the bitter cold. I have been taken from my family and placed with strangers. I have been insulted, attacked, mugged, raped, and murdered by the descendants of settlers my ancestors . . . survived . . . I have decided to end my life

---

[7] Vi Waln, 'Healing your trauma', *Teton Times* 17, no. 31, (June 19-June 26), 4.

. . .'[8] Advertisements for therapy for people suffering from historical trauma and suicidal thoughts addressed to people 'from ages 12 and up', suggest that the feelings of the Lakota Teen are not unique.

The impact of 'Indian invisibility', referred to by the Lakota Teen, is also not unique. For example, debates about reparations for African American slavery and Japanese American internment play out in contemporary media. Unheard are discussions about restitution for injustices suffered by Native Americans. Although genocide is on the list, Indian claims focus on the death, disease, and environmental contamination resulting from radiation poisoning dating back to the 1940s nuclear experiments in Los Alamos, New Mexico.

The attack on Indian bodies and environments continued with uranium mining from the 1950s through the 1970s in New Mexico, Colorado, Arizona, Utah, and Washington State.[9] It reached its peak with the Church Rock nuclear spill in 1979, second in magnitude only to the Chernobyl melt-down. The radiation fall-out and uranium dust sickened people and animals, and contaminated land, water, and air. And still does. Radiation is linked to the miscarriages, birth defects, and debilitating arthritis plaguing Indian country. It also causes the cancers and diabetes that are the number-one killers of Native Americans.[10]

---

[8] Brian Keller, 'I am a Lakota Teen', *Teton Times* 17, no. 31, (June 19-June 26), 4.
[9] 'High uranium levels seen in Navajo women decades after Cold War era mining by U.S. on their reservation', *CBS News*, October 8, 2019, https://www.cbsnews.com/news/high-uranium-levels-seen-in-navajo-women-decades-after-cold-war-era-mining-by-u-s-on-their-reservation/.
[10] Interview of Geneal Anderson in Carole Gallagher, *American Ground Zero: The Secret Nuclear War* (NY: Random House, 1993), 206-208; 'Professor Elizabeth Hoover on Food Sovereignty, Mines and Pipelines', interview by Paul DeMain, *News from Indian Country,* April 30, 2019, https://www.indiancountrynews.com/index.php/columnists/paul-demain/14719-professor-elizabeth-hoover-on-food-sovereignty-mines-and-pipelines; Dorothy Purley, 'Uranium Mining and the Laguna People', interview by Susan Lee, July 1995 in Paguate Village on the Laguna Pueblo Reservation, *Synthesis/Regeneration* 10 (Spring 1996).

But Indian cries for reparations are ignored. Why would people react to demands for 'pay back' for something that, according to the silences in American history textbooks, did not happen? Unseen in the past, radiation fall-out and uranium contamination remain unknown in the present.

The dominant narrative of American history is linear. Popular textbooks used in universities internationally unfold chronologically. They typically begin with Colonial America and end with modern times. Knowledge gleaned from one decade informs understanding of the next. Concluding paragraphs raise questions about future possibilities. Similarly, 'the' news, in its many platforms, focuses on the present. The tendency is to feature historical moments and developments within the context of commemoration. Native narratives tell different histories that testify to the presence of the past.

References

Brook, Daniel. 'Environmental Genocide: Native Americans and Toxic Waste'. *The American Journal of Economics and Sociology* 57, no. 1 (1998): 105-13.

Brugge, Doug, and Esther Yazzie-Lewis. *The Navajo People and Uranium Mining*. Edited by Doug Brugge and Timothy Benally. Albuquerque: University of New Mexico Press, 2006.

Dewar, Dale, Linda Harvey, and Cathy Vakil. 'Uranium Mining and Health'. *Can Fam Physician* 59, no. 5 (2013): 469-471.

Fonseca, Felicia. 'Tribes Press Government to Clean Up Nuclear Waste'. *Indian Country*, June 2009. https://www.indiancountrynews.com/index.php/news/politcs-business/6639-tribes-press-government-to-clean-up-nuclear-waste.

Fox, Sarah Alisabeth. *Downwind: A People's History of the Nuclear West*. Lincoln: Bison Books, 2018.

Fuchs, Miriam and Craig Howes. *Teaching Life Writing Texts*. New York: The Modern Language Association of America, 2008.

Holmes, Sue M. 'Navajos Mark 30th Anniversary of Uranium Spill'. *Indian Country*, July 27, 2009. https://www.indiancountrynews.com/index.php/news/indian-and-first-nations/7045-navajos-mark-30th-anniversary-of-uranium-spill.

Hoover, Elizabeth, Katsi Cook, Ron Plain, Kathy Sanchez, Vi Waghiyi, Pamela Miller, Renee Dufault, Caitlin Sislin, and David O. Carpenter. 'Indigenous Peoples of North America: Environmental Exposures and Reproductive Justice'. *Environmental Health* 120, no. 12 (2012). https://ehp.niehs.nih.gov/doi/10.1289/ehp.1205422.

Justice, Daniel Heath, 'No Indian Is an Island: On the Ethics of Teaching Indigenous Life Writing Texts', In *Teaching Life Writing Texts*, edited by Miriam Fuchs and Craig Howes, 255. New York: The Modern Language Association of America, 2008.

Smith, Sidonie and Julia Watson, eds. *Women, Autobiography, Theory: A Reader.* Madison: University of Wisconsin Press, 1998.

Smith, Sidonie and Julia Watson, eds. *Autobiography Studies Reader: Life Writing in the Long Run.* Ann Arbor: Michigan Publishing, 2016.

Voyles, Traci Brynne. *Wastelanding: Legacies of Uranium Mining in Navajo Country*. Minneapolis: University of Minnesota Press, 2015.

Hardly Seen, Unheard, Unspoken:
A Response to Dr. Nancy Mykoff

Léa Jörg & Taylor Lee

When we first read through Dr. Mykoff's outline, we were surprised by its contents. Of course, we've heard of the Native American struggles before. They are fighting constantly to have their voices heard and their land and traditions preserved. But we were honestly unaware of many facets of their struggles; the literal poisoning of indigenous land and indigenous lives was new to us. These three aspects you touched upon, seen, but only in certain aspects. Unheard and unspoken, they are important aspects of the daily lives of indigenous peoples. In our response, we would like to build upon what we think is a recurring narrative: indigenous peoples are seen, but only in certain, limited ways. Their struggles and voices remain unheard and unspoken. This ties into their health, but also their lands. It is the latter that we will focus on, in particular the Dakota Access Pipeline in the United States, and the Energía Eólica del Sur wind park in Mexico.

The Dakota Access Pipeline is a 1,200 mi, or 1,900 km, long underground crude oil pipeline that transports oil from North Dakota through South Dakota and Iowa into Illinois.[1] Discussions for this pipeline started in 2014 when the local public was informed. The construction began in June 2016 and the pipeline became operational in June 2017. Protests began in the spring of 2016 and were largely conducted by Native Americans, specifically the Sioux Nation and the Standing Rock tribe.[2] They were concerned about their environmental and economic wellbeing and how that might be affected by the pipeline.

---

[1] Dakota Access Pipeline Facts, 'Home'.
[2] AP News, 'Timeline of the Dakota Access Oil Pipeline'.

Furthermore, they were concerned about how sites of great historical, religious, and cultural significance might be affected by this pipeline. The protesters called themselves 'Water Protectors', as the pipeline was planned to go through Lake Oahe, the primary water source of the Standing Rock tribe. This directly led to the largest gathering of American Indians in the past century.

Another example of the protest narrative was 'ReZpect Our Water', led by young American Indian youth in July 2016. They physically ran from Standing Rock in North Dakota and South Dakota to Washington D.C. in protest of the pipeline.[3] We can see that this pipeline is an example of environmental racism against American Indians in the fact that the pipeline was originally going to be located approximately 16 kms northeast of Bismarck, North Dakota, the second-largest city in North Dakota and 92% white. Later, the pipeline was moved to the very boundary of Sioux Standing Rock territory due to the threat posed to the Bismarck water supply. In the media, this is portrayed first through the Dakota Access Pipeline website, DAPLPipelineFacts.com. You can't access it in the Netherlands, but luckily, I have a VPN for streaming on my parents' U.S. accounts so I was able to access this website. The website states that the Dakota Access Pipeline doesn't encroach or cross any land of the Standing Rock tribe.[4] However, the Standing Rock tribe combats this, citing the Fort Laramie Treaty of 1868 which grants more land (including that through which the pipeline travels) than the present-day reservation to the Sioux Nation as well as the 1980 U.S. Supreme Court determination that the land was stolen illegally from Native American tribes, among many other areas.[5] Furthermore, the pipeline website argues that the oil pipeline does not encroach on

---

[3] Greene, 'ReZpect'.
[4] Dakota Access Pipeline Facts, 'The Facts'.
[5] Hasselman, 'Plaintiff Standing Rock Sioux Tribe's Memorandum'; Native Knowledge 360° 'Treaties Still Matter'.

the water supply of the Standing Rock tribe.[6] This is because they forced the Native Americans to move their water intake location 50 kms further away and the pipeline now passes below the Missouri River and Lake Oahe.[7] The DAPL website also links to two other websites, both of which are fact-checkers; one by Snopes and one by a blogger. There is a common narrative on these websites: Instead of calling the Standing Rock protesters 'Water Protectors', Native Americans, activists, or any such positive terms, they are referred to consistently and repetitively as 'eco-terrorists'.[8]

There was international attention for the Dakota Access Pipeline and protests before there was any in the U.S. media. The latter didn't discuss the Dakota Access Pipeline until September 2016, when workers bulldozed a section of land that was documented by Sioux Historical Preservation officers as a historical and sacred site.[9] This also led to the National Day of Action on November 15th in different cities across America and the world.[10] These efforts proved pointless, as on January 24th President Trump approved the advancement of the Dakota Access Pipeline's development, blockading further environmental restrictions put upon it.[11] So, while this movement did gain momentum in the media, it only delayed the pipeline. It could not stop it. Even when it was portrayed in the media, it was primarily non-American Indians talking about American Indians, their land, and their heritage. One such example: Swedish activist Greta Thunberg traveling to Standing Rock as a featured speaker.[12]

[6] 'The Facts'.
[7] Cohn, 'The Human Right'.
[8] Snopes.com, 'Standing Rock Archives'; Standing Rock Fact Checker, 'Midwest Alliance for Infrastructure Now'.
[9] McCauley, "Is That Not Genocide?'.
[10] Schleeter, '#NoDAPL Day of Action'; Goodman, 'Dakota Access Pipeline Protests Spread'.
[11] Jones, Diamon, and Krieg, 'Trump Advances Keystone Pipeline'.
[12] Sisk, 'Teen Climate Activists'.

I'd like to argue that this is not solely a case of cultural heritage or environmental activism and racism, but rather that they are one and the same and work together within the Native American narrative.

Our second example of the seen-unheard-unspoken narrative is, in our opinion, a global phenomenon. The Energía Eólica del Sur is a wind park situated in the state of Oaxaca in Mexico. It is the largest wind park in Latin America at the moment, with 132 wind turbines that are working.[13] The wind park provides clean energy, which is great. If you have ever been to a climate march before, you have probably heard the chant, 'Hey hey, ho ho, fossil fuels have got to go', and this is exactly what Mexico is trying to achieve through Energía Eólica del Sur. The wind park is situated in the Isthmus of Tehuantepec, which is the narrowest strip of land between the Atlantic and Pacific Oceans, so there is a lot of wind. It is the perfect space for wind turbines.

However, there is a catch: It is also the land of the Zapotec people, one of the many indigenous groups of Mexico. They have been attempting to stop the project from becoming a reality since its beginnings. There have been conflicts of interest between indigenous groups and leaders of the project. For instance, it was clear that the project would cut down 100% of the forested area without proposing compensatory measures, and there was an insufficient assessment of the impact of the windfarm.[14] Still, the wind park has been inaugurated in May of this year and portrayed in the national news from *La Jornada* as a collaboration between indigenous villages in the area and the state. The federal administration 'would respect the voice' of the Zapotec people. However, this clearly has not happened. The 'Wind Energy Megaproject' of the Isthmus of Tehuantepec has already created social schisms and conflict in

---

[13] Manzo and Pérez, 'Inauguran en Oaxaca'.
[14] Garcia Feria, 'Wind Power and Environmental Justice', 87–102.

indigenous communities.[15] The projects in this region resemble an extractive model, which are managed top-down to the detriment of local communities. Furthermore, those projects can have adverse effects on the local biodiversity.[16]

The Zapotec have been fishers for a long time and depend on fishing for material and spiritual sustenance. This way of providing food is a large part of their heritage, which they now struggle to transmit with the construction of wind parks. There are deep concerns about pollution through the construction and sustenance of turbines, and how noise and vibrations could affect marine life.[17] Furthermore, the witnessing of mass killings of fish during the construction of pilot wind turbines led to uprisings in the local communities.[18] Their lands are forever altered by the construction and implementation of this wind park. A final aspect to take into consideration: The Zapotec people get no financial benefit from the project, nor can they access the energy that is produced through the wind turbines, despite living in the same region. The Zapotecs are seen by the Mexican government and by multi-national corporations because their presence cannot be ignored. Yet, their reality clashes with the lucrative business of creating 'green energy'. Their struggles are still unheard, even though they are trying to speak up. Many things remain unspoken. This is an example of what I would call a transnational, indigenous struggle because the struggles that the Standing Rock Tribe and the Zapotecs face share the same characteristics of social and environmental destruction, even though those people have no direct relation to each other.

By looking at those three examples of Dr. Mykoff's discussion on Native Americans, Taylor's contribution with the Standing Rock

---

[15] Toledo, Patiño, and Fraga, 'Justice', 1.
[16] Garcia Feria, 'Wind Power and Environmental Justice'.
[17] Dunlap, 'The 'Solution'', 550-73.
[18] Dunlap, 560.

Tribe, and Léa's discussion on the Zapotecs, we'd like to conclude that we see a correlation in their struggles – that are hardly seen, unheard, and unspoken. While visibility has increased through media and popularity, the actions that should follow up are still not a reality. Because of this, we call for future research into and awareness of the relationship between environmental activism and cultural heritage. We would also like to make a personal call for action in support of these unheard indigenous voices. In conclusion, we find that being seen does not yet equal being heard, but it is the first step.

References

AP NEWS. 'A Timeline of the Dakota Access Oil Pipeline'. October 12, 2017. https://apnews.com article/1a00f95c83594dac931796a332540750.

Cohn, Marjorie. 'The Human Right to Water at Standing Rock'. *Truthout*, November 3, 2016. https://truthout.org/articles/the-human-right-to-water-at-standing-rock/.

Dunlap, Alexander. 'The 'Solution' Is Now the 'Problem:' Wind Energy, Colonisation and the 'Genocide-Ecocide Nexus' in the Isthmus of Tehuantepec, Oaxaca'. *The International Journal of Human Rights* 22, no. 4 (April 21, 2018): 550–73. https://doi.org/10.1080/13642987.2017.1397633.

Garcia Feria, Yajaira. 'Wind Power and Environmental Justice: The Case of Istmo de Tehuantepec'. In *Green Crime in Mexico: A Collection of Case Studies*, edited by Ines Arroyo-Quiroz and Tanya Wyatt, 87–102. Cham: Springer International Publishing, 2018. https://doi.org/10.1007/978-3-319-75286-0_7.

Goodman, Amy. 'Dakota Access Pipeline Protests Spread to 300 Cities as Pipeline Owner Sues to Continue Construction'. *Democracy Now!*, November 16, 2016. http://www.democracynow.org/2016/11/16/nodapl_protests_spread_to_300_cities.

Greene, Eleanor. 'ReZpect Our Water'. *Green America*, Fall 2017. https://www.greenamerica.org/drinking-water-risk/rezpect-our-water.

Hasselman, Jan E. 'Plaintiff Standing Rock Sioux Tribe's Memorandum in Support of its Motion for Partial Summary Judgment'. Pub. L. No. 1:16-cv-1534-JEB, 47 (2017). https://earthjustice.org/sites/default/files/files/Memo-ISO-SRSTs-Mtn-for-PSJ.pdf.

Dakota Access Pipeline Facts. 'Home'. Accessed October 24, 2019. https://www.daplpipelinefacts.com.

Jones, Athena, Jeremy Diamon, and Gregory Krieg. 'Trump Advances Keystone Pipeline, DAPL with Executive Actions'. *CNN*, January 24, 2017. http://www.cnn.com/2017/01/24/politics/trump-keystone-xl-dakota-access-pipelines-executive-actions/index.html.

Manzo, Diana, and Jorge A. Pérez. 'Inauguran en Oaxaca el Parque Eólico del Sur - Estados - La Jornada'. *La Jornada*, May 29, 2019. https://www.jornada.com.mx/ultimas/estados/2019/05/29/inauguran-en-oaxaca-el-parque-eolico-del-sur-6621.html.

McCauley, Lauren. "Is That Not Genocide?' Pipeline Co. Bulldozing Burial Sites Prompts Emergency Motion'. *Common Dreams*, September 5, 2016. https://www.commondreams.org/news/2016/09/05/not-genocide-pipeline-co-bulldozing-burial-sites-prompts-emergency-motion.

Midwest Alliance for Infrastructure Now. 'Standing Rock Fact Checker'. Standing Rock Fact Checker. Accessed October 24, 2019. https://standingrockfactchecker.org/.

Schleeter, Ryan. '#NoDAPL Day of Action Draws Tens of Thousands, Lights Up Social Media'. *Greenpeace USA* (blog), November 16, 2016. https://www.greenpeace.org/usa/nodapl-day-action-draws-tens-thousands-lights-social-media/.

Sisk, Amy R. 'Teen Climate Activists Speak on Standing Rock Sioux Reservation'. *Bismarck Tribune*, October 8, 2019. https://bismarcktribune.com/news/state-and-regional/teen-climate-activists-speak-on-standing-rock-sioux-reservation/article_f70eecb7-f0c6-53d1-bd0c-bfdc3db7005d.html.

Snopes.com. 'Standing Rock Archives'. Accessed October 24, 2019. https://www.snopes.com/tag/standing-rock/.

Dakota Access Pipeline Facts. 'The Facts'. Accessed October 24, 2019. https://www.daplpipelinefacts.com/The-Facts.html.

Native Knowledge 360°. 'Treaties Still Matter: The Dakota Access Pipeline'. Accessed October 24, 2019. http://nmai.si.edu/nk360/plains-treaties/dapl.cshtml.

Zárate-Toledo, Ezequiel, Rodrigo Patiño, and Julia Fraga. 'Justice, Social Exclusion and Indigenous Opposition: A Case Study of Wind Energy Development on the Isthmus of Tehuantepec, Mexico'. *Energy Research & Social Science* 54 (August 1, 2019): 1–11. https://doi.org/10.1016/j.erss.2019.03.004.

'Kandy is now Flanders': Maps as Visual Heritage in the First Dutch Envoy to Ceylon, 1602-1604

Danielle Gravon

At the center of the map of Ceylon from Johann Theodor De Bry's abridged version of *'t Historiael Journael* are two kneeling worshipers who flank the Buddhist deity Ganesh.[1] The idol draws attention to the Kandy court, a Sinhalese stronghold Portuguese and Dutch colonizers sought to conquer. Moving away from Kandy, the landscape is stippled with Buddhist pagodas, Catholic churches, and Portuguese fortifications.[2] At the bottom is a Grand Pagoda, framed by worshipers, and the mountain *Sri Pada*, which is labelled in Portuguese as Adam's Peak. The site was long-venerated by Buddhists and Hindus, who believed the foot-shaped indent on its top belonged to Buddha and Shiva respectively. It was appropriated by Christian colonizers, who claimed the imprint was Adam's.[3]

By mirroring the Grand Pagoda with the Christianized Adam's Peak, the map points to passages in the original travel account that compare Catholic and Buddhist religious art as idolatrous. Through aesthetic comparisons, the volume constructs Dutch heritage in opposition to these 'heathenish' religions. It grounds

---

[1] *Zelon* is the map's title. This refers to present-day Sri Lanka. *'t Historiael Journael* switches between the spellings Zelon, Ceylon, Celon, and Zeilan. To avoid confusion, I use Ceylon unless it is spelled otherwise in a quotation or image. Joris van Spilbergen, *'t Historiael journael van tghene ghepasseert is van weghen drie schepen, ghenaemt den Ram, Schaep ende t' Lam: ghevaren wt Zeelant vander stadt Camp-Vere, naer d'Oost- Indien, onder tbeleyt van Joris van Speilberghen generael, anno 1601. den 5. Mey, tot in t'eylant Celon, vervatende veel schoone geschiedenissen, die by haer op dese reyse gheschiedt zijn, inden tijdt van twee jaer elff maenden, neghentien daghen* (Delft, Floris Balthasars, 1605).
[2] *'T Historiael Journael* switches between the spellings Candi, Candy, and Kandy for the indigenous name of the city. I use Kandy, as it is typically spelled today, unless it is spelled otherwise in a quotation or image.
[3] Holt, ed., *The Sri Lanka Reader,* 171–3.

Dutch identity in Calvinist ideologies, with particular concern afforded to images and their use. The uncharacteristically blank cartouche prompts questions about the volume's original context, offering entry into how publishers were constructing, adapting, and disseminating ideas of heritage to different audiences.

The original map was published in *'t Historiael Journael*, a travel account detailing the first Dutch envoy to Ceylon from 1602 to 1604 led by the Reformed Antwerp-native Joris van Spilbergen. The account was kept by Cornelis Jansz Vennip and other members of the crew after his death.[4] It was published in Delft in 1605 by Balthasar Floris van Berckenrode, also a Protestant, who fled Flanders for Zeeland during the Eighty Years' War. The account is paired with a summary of Portuguese-Sinhalese relations leading up to Dutch arrival in Ceylon. This understudied travel narrative is a rich source that frames the Dutch-Sinhalese encounter in light of contemporary discourses on Dutch independence and visual culture during the Reformation.[5]

I ask: How does *'t Historiael Journael* play an active role in constructing Dutch heritage through pictures and discussions of visual culture and what were the implications of De Bry's alterations to the abridged version he published in *India Orientalis* in 1613? By analyzing the text and images in this book and positioning the account in relation to other cartographic projects commissioned by

---

[4] K. D. Paranavitana, trans., 'Introduction', 1.

[5] I have used Paranavitana's English translation of *'t Historiael Journael*. Where no translation is extant, as is the case with the image inscriptions and the dedicatory text, or where issues in translation arise, a transcription of the original is provided. Paranavitana gives important background about the volume, but does not offer a critical analysis. R. K. de Silva and W. G. M. Beumer's *Illustrations and Views of Dutch Ceylon 1602–1796* provides a summary of *'t Historiael Journael*, but it does not offer a critical interpretation of the work.

leaders of the early Republic, I suggest that the Dutch conceived of religious and cartographic images as opposing modes of representation and were actively constructing Dutch heritage using maps.[6] De Bry, however, neutralised the polemic rhetoric of the original. The popularity of De Bry's *India Orientalis* over *'t Historiael Journael* concealed the original's place in this larger program of Dutch cartographic propaganda. While this paper does not focus on digital heritage, it is important to note that I was able to recover this history because digital technologies enabled me to compare these materials that exist in different collections across the world.

Spilbergen arrived in Ceylon on the 31st of May 1602 with three ships from the company of Balthazar de Moucheron, another Reformed Calvinist from Antwerp, who fled after playing a crucial role in negotiating the city's surrender. The ships approach from the south with the caption: 'Here is where we first sighted land: we sailed forward to Matecalo'.[7] Dotted lines extend along the coast, marking the path taken to find a strategic landing away from the Portuguese. A figure on shore illustrates the meeting of Spilbergen and the King of Matecalo. During this encounter, Spilbergen was accused of being Portuguese. He managed 'with great difficulty' to make 'the King believe otherwise, whereupon he obtained his freedom'.[8] This did not quell the King's suspicion. The following

---

[6] This paper builds on Svetlana Alpers's notion of the 'mapping impulse' in 17th-century Dutch art, which she characterizes as, 'an impulse to record or describe the land in pictures that was shared at the time by surveyors, artists, printers, and the general public in the Netherlands'. Importantly, Alpers blurs the anachronistic boundaries between the disciplines of cartography and art. Controversially, she maintains that the descriptive approach to art making in the north was distinctive from the narrative art of Renaissance Italy. I build on her concept by using *'t Historiael Journael* to bring Dutch maps into broader aesthetic discourses, with special regard for religious and non-European visual cultures, which her study does not cover. See Alpers, 'The Mapping Impulse in Dutch Art' in *The Art of Describing: Dutch Art in the Seventeenth Century*, 119-68, esp. 147.

[7] 'Hier is ons 't lant oerst ontdeckt syn voort naer Maticala geseilt.'

[8] Spilbergen, *Journal of Spilbergen*, 23.

day Spilbergen 'once again explained that neither he nor his people were Portuguese but Zeelanders'.[9] Such a misunderstanding was made easily enough, considering Spilbergen conversed in Portuguese, the diplomatic language of royal Ceylon.[10] This early description sets the tone for the rest of the travel account, in which the Dutch position themselves in opposition to the Portuguese, a maneuver directed as much towards the account's intended Dutch audience as it was to the indigenous rulers of Ceylon.

The cartouche in the original introduces some of the main characters involved in producing *'t Historiael Journael*: 'This journal of a sea voyage to India is dedicated by Balthazar Floris of Delft, publisher to the illustrious and mighty gentlemen of Zeeland and to the most illustrious Maurice of Nassau, Prince of Orange and Admiral of the sea'.[11] De Moucheron, whose company financed and provided ships for the journey, established a relationship with Prince Maurice long before Spilbergen set sail. De Moucheron won Prince Maurice's support for earlier attempts to establish trade routes to Asia.[12] The map's dedication implies he offered similar support, as does Spilbergen's claim to be negotiating on his behalf.

The publisher, Berckenrode, was also well-acquainted with Prince Maurice. He worked in his service and in the States General's from 1599 to 1617.[13] He began by making siege maps in collaboration with Hugo Grotius, the famed political theorist from Delft. These maps illustrate the Dutch capture of Netherlandish cities from the Habsburgs, like this one of *The Battle at Nieuwpoort*. Siege maps were popular news maps, appearing as broadsides and in pamphlets

[9] Spilbergen, 23.
[10] De Silva, *Portuguese Encounters*, xxii.
[11] 'Illustribus potentibusque DD. Ordinibus Zelandia, and Illustrissimo D. Mauritio Nassavio Principi Arausiorum etc. Praefecto Maris etc. Diarium hoc Indice navigationis consecrat Florentius Balthazari F. Delph: editor.'
[12] Spies, *Arctic Routes*, 19; Zandvliet, *Mapping for Money*, 34.
[13] Lynam, 'Floris Balthasar', 158–61; Zandvliet, 'Kartografie', 17–50.

of war propaganda.[14] Siege maps were also included in early Dutch historiographies.[15] Forty appear in Jan Janszoon Orlers's *The Triumphs of Nassau* from 1610, and there are many more like this. Siege maps, then, were not only important for the present political moment, but also in fashioning Dutch historical consciousness. Berckenrode confirms the importance of images in *'t Historiael Journael*'s dedication: 'It would be reprehensible and lamentable, that if there were devout and brave men in a country, no history writers or engravers would appear, by whom the deeds of these men would be reported to future generations'.[16] Berckenrode establishes the travel account as part of a greater effort to construct Dutch heritage through text and images. This image of *The Battle at Nieuwpoort* will emerge again, when Spilbergen describes this battle to the Kandy King.

During the Twelve Years' Truce, when siege maps were no longer necessary, Berckenrode was commissioned to produce survey maps of Dutch territories.[17] These were important for defining the still-contested borders of the young republic. While the Seven United Provinces was established in 1579 with the Union of Utrecht, it was not formally recognized by the Habsburgs until 1648 with the Peace of Münster.[18] It was during this interim period, in which the leaders of the Republic declared independence without acknowledgment, that they initiated this vigorous map-making program. Many of the figures involved in the production of siege maps, survey maps, and *'t Historiael Journael* shared a common experience of religious

---

[14] Hooijdonk, 'News, Propaganda', 132– 62 (at pp. 137–9); Donkersloot-De Vrij, *The World*, 34; Lynam, 158–61; and Liedtke, *Vermeer*, 191.
[15] Hooijdonk, 135.
[16] Original text from Joris van Spilbergen, *'t Historiael Journael* , p. iii: 'Also vvare het van glijcke berispelijck ende beclaechlijck, dat vvanneer in eenich landt vrome coene Mannen te zijn, metter daedt bevvesen vverdt, daer geen Histori- schrijvers ofte Plaet-snijders te voorschijn en quamen, door de vvelcke der voorsz mannen daden den nacomelinghen medeghedeylt wirden.'
[17] van den Brink, 'De kaart van Rijnland', 1–16.
[18] Manzano Baena, *Conflicting Words*, 163–72.

persecution and forced migration, which united them in the ambitions to shape the ideologies and aesthetic identity of the early Republic through print.

The quantity and variety of cartographic projects backed by Dutch leaders of the early Republic suggest that maps were integral to how they sought to shape and preserve this historical moment for future generations. Their preference for maps over religious imagery is confirmed in *'t Historiael Journael*. The account is not only accompanied by numerous maps, but the text frequently compares and criticizes Buddhist and Catholic styles and their use of images in worship. After realizing he was negotiating with the wrong king, Spilbergen set off to meet the King of Kandy, jotting down observations along the way. The envoys travelled through the town of Vintane, marked on *Zelon* with a small pagoda. The town plan shows they were greeted with a ceremony. Spilbergen and his men approach in the foreground. Musicians, monks, soldiers, and elephants process through the streets towards the focal point – a large pagoda in the town's center. The text vividly describes a 'very beautiful and high' pagoda that is 'all white with a gilded top and built like a pyramid, rising upwards oval wise to a four-cornered point'.[19] It moves to a description of the monastery, marked with an '8' in the top right corner. The monastery is described as 'similar to those of ours in this country, surrounded by galleries and many private chapels which are gilded and contain many figures of men and women whom they say have lived holy lives'.[20] Spilbergen's comparative observations then take a critical turn: 'When one observes these customs and habits of the monks in monasteries and in processions, one would certainly think that our monks had learned most of their ceremonies from these heathens'.[21]

---

[19] Spilbergen, *Journal of Spilbergen*, 28.
[20] Spilbergen, 28.
[21] Spilbergen, 29.

While heathen was typically used to describe non-Christians, during the period Catholics and Reformists alike used the term to refer to one another. This is clear in a letter by de Moucheron to fellow merchant Olivier Brunel, exclaiming 'there are more heathens in the world, even right here in Antwerp'.[22]

When he finally arrived at the Kandy Court, he noted that all the King's new buildings were constructed according to the 'Christian style'.[23] The Great Hall was decorated with 'Spanish chairs' and a table arranged in the 'Christian manner'.[24] The King and his family were dressed in the 'Christian manner' too.[25] The text never defines what is meant by Christian style or manner, but the use of Spanish and Portuguese as synonyms and the earlier comparison of Catholic and Buddhist art, suggests that Christian refers to a distinctly ornate Catholic aesthetic.

During their weeks together, King Vimaladharmasuriya I of Kandy gave Spilbergen tours through his 'many and costly pagodas'.[26] The text observes that the pagodas 'had more than four or five thousand carved figures, some of them as high as masts, for which extraordinary and ingenious towers have expressly been made of fine stone. They are all vaulted and gilt, and indeed their pagodas far surpass the Popish churches in architecture'.[27] At one point in their discussions, the Kandy King requested Spilbergen's opinion of his pagodas and asked how they compared to his own. This presented Spilbergen with an opportunity to compare the visual cultures of Sinhalese Buddhism, Portuguese Catholicism, and Dutch Reformism to Dutch audiences through a conversation with the King:

[22] Spies, *Artic Routes*, 116; De Stoppelaar, *Balthasar de Moucheron*, 23–4.
[23] Spilbergen, *Journal of Spilbergen*, 39.
[24] Spilbergen, 31.
[25] Spilbergen, 32.
[26] Spilbergen, 31.
[27] Spilbergen, 31.

The King asked him whether our pagodas were also like those of the Portuguese, adorned with images such as Maria, Petro, and Paulo, and others, and whether we too believed in Christ. The General answered that we were true Christians in faith not Popish Roman Catholics like the Portuguese. The king also wished to be informed of what we had in our Churches. The General showed him the bare wall and said that we had the true God in our hearts who had created heaven and earth and all of us. He was further admonished that he should not rely on pagodas, but on God who had created everything, which the King understood well and pointed to his palace and the city and said: 'All this has God given to me'.[28]

Spilbergen's position on religious images as useless and idolatrous is no surprise considering he was a Reformed Calvinist, as were the others involved in producing *'t Historiael Journael*. The journal claims that Spilbergen and the Kandy King spent five entire days in each other's company, having various discussions 'too long to be narrated here'.[29] This passing comment suggests that their conversations concerning religious imagery were deliberately concocted as an integral part of the travel account, reinforcing just how much the construction of early Dutch identity and heritage was informed by Reformation image debates.

The account says that at end of his stay in Kandy, Spilbergen gifted a portrait of Prince Maurice to King Vimaladharmasuriya. Unfortunately, the painting is lost, but a print offers us a good example, particularly because the Battle of Nieuwpoort is pictured in the background. The journal describes an image, in which Prince

---

[28] Spilbergen, 31.
[29] Spilbergen, 31.

Maurice sits on 'horseback in full saddle in the form and the size of the horse and the person as he appeared at the battle in Flanders on 2nd July 1602', no doubt referring to the Battle of Nieuwpoort.[30] Spilbergen described the battle and the 'position of [the] United Netherlands, and also how the States General continued that war against the King of Portugal and Spain under the leadership of His Excellency the Prince'.[31] The telling of this battle and gift of Prince Maurice's portrait was a means of convincing the King of Kandy that the Dutch were true allies. Furthermore, it serves to canonize this battle in the struggle for Dutch sovereignty. Berckenrode's engraving of *The Battle at Nieuwpoort* is a testament to this. The siege map depicts the Dutch army, under the command of Prince Maurice, fighting against the Spanish, led by Albert Archduke of Austria. Prince Maurice's forces organize on the right and the Archduke's on the left, where they meet in a fierce, chaotic battle in the middle. The text in the bottom left, crowned with victory flanked by two *Leones Belgici*, contains the poetry of Grotius, who narrates the event with praise for the guidance of Prince Maurice in defeating the Archduke. While this battle did little to further the Dutch agenda, Berckenrode's map pictures it as a pivotal victory for the Dutch Republic, as does *'t Historiael Journael*.

The cursive lettering, the line quality of the shaded figures, and the bird's-eye view share the same characteristics of Berckenrode's town plans and map in the travel account. Using comparable visual tropes, like the coat of arms of Prince Maurice and the provinces and dedications to Dutch leaders, Berckenrode's siege map finds its counterpart in the map of Ceylon. The Dutch-Ceylonese alliance was sealed by the Kandy King. The text says: 'The King, with his Prince and Princess, began to learn the Dutch language, saying that Candy is now Flanders'.[32] That Kandy would be Flanders

---

[30] This date refers to the Battle at Nieuwpoort, and thus 1602 is a misprint that should read 1600. Spilbergen, 31-32.
[31] Spilbergen, 32.
[32] Spilbergen, 32.

and not Zeeland, suggests the authors were nostalgic to recover a lost territory, a home land. It implies that the Kandy King simply handed over his territory to Spilbergen.[33] This is represented in the way the Dutch put themselves on the map of Ceylon – not with settlements, but coats of arms and cartouches that visually encapsulate the island and a homophone title that imposes Zeeland onto *Zelon*.

The travel account was printed several more times throughout the century – in Dutch, Latin, and German.[34] It gained wide appeal outside the Dutch Republic in De Bry's collection of voyages, *India Orientalis*. While the travel account was included, Berckenrode's dedication to the States General and the history of Portuguese-Sinhalese relations were omitted. De Bry cut these sections, because these texts unfavorably represented the Portuguese and papacy. While not all of the anti-Catholic elements were removed during this process, many extracts were significantly altered.

A key example of this appears in the Latin text published in 1613, in which no term to designate heathen was included in the passage comparing Sinhalese and Catholic monks and monasteries.[35] De Bry manipulated the original text and images to suit a confessionally divided readership.

---

[33] The English translation of this passage suggests this was expressed in Dutch, but the original Dutch text, which uses oblique strokes (/) to divide phrases, is more ambiguous. See, Hexham, *Het groot woordenboeck gestalt in 't Neder-duytsch, ende in 't Engelsch.*

[34] Three Dutch versions were published before the Spanish formally recognised the Dutch Republic with the Peace of Westphalia in 1648. They were reproduced in Amsterdam by Michiel Colijn in 1617 and 1619 and by Joannes Janssonius in 1646. Versions after the Peace of Westphalia include those by Joost Hartegers in 1648 and 1652 and by Gillis Joosten Saeghman, but the year of publication is not indicated in the latter. See, Spilbergen, *Journal of Spilbergen*, 9; Muller, *Catalogue*, 168.

[35] De Bry, ed., *India Orientalis pars septem*, 22.

These alterations were part of an editorial strategy intended to target multiple book markets.[36]

Visual analysis and measurements show that De Bry's engravings were not printed using the original plates, although they appear to be carefully copied, with the exception of parts of the map. In terms of place names and topographical features, De Bry's version is similar to the original. The Dutch text has been removed, except in two instances near the place-names Manar and Setavacco, where it has been translated into German.[37] The most significant difference between the two maps is that in De Bry's version the coats of arms of Prince Maurice and Zeeland have been entirely erased. The cartouche in the bottom right corner, dedicating this map to leaders of the Dutch Republic, remains blank. By omitting crucial pieces of the text, modifying others, and erasing details in the map, De Bry neutralizes the polemic language of 't Historiael Journael. These changes concealed the map's initial function as pro-Republic propaganda, refashioning this history in the process. The popularity of De Bry's work over the original, which is evident from the fact that hundreds of copies of the former still exist while only two of the latter remain, further obscures this history.

In conclusion, the evidence shows that 't Historiael Journael was part of a greater initiative by the leaders of the Dutch Republic to shape

---

[36] This argument was made by Michiel van Groesen in his lengthy analysis of the De Bry's publication of travel narratives. His argument provides a constructive way to engage with the changes De Bry made to 't Historiael Journael. See, van Groesen, The Representations of the Overseas World in the De Bry collection of Voyage (1590-1634).
[37] The original Dutch is: 'Setavacco is een groote stadt daer de coninc van Celon syn hof houdt.' The German reads: 'Setavacco ist ein große Stat de der Konig von Celon sein hof helt.' The English translation: 'Setavacco is a great city, where the king of Ceylon holds court.' The original Dutch is: 'Hier is een visserij van paerlle.' The German is: 'Hir ist ein fischerey von parlen.' The English translation: 'Here is a pearl fishery.'

a geographically, politically, and religiously unified Dutch identity, of which maps were a key facet. The original aim of the work as explicit propaganda was smoothed over by De Bry's alterations and concealed by the popularity of his work over the original.

References

Alpers, Svetlana. *The Art of Describing: Dutch Art in the Seventeenth Century*. Chicago: University of Chicago Press, 1983.

De Bry, Johann Theodor de Bry. T. *India Orientalis pars septem*. Translated by G. Arthus. Frankfurt: Johann Theodor de Bry, 1613.

De Silva, R. K. and Beumer, W. G. M. *Illustrations and Views of Dutch Ceylon 1602–1796: A Comprehensive Work of Pictorial Reference with Selected Eye-witness Accounts*. Leiden: Brill, 1988.

De Silva, Chandra R. *Portuguese Encounters with Sri Lanka and the Maldives: Translated Texts from the Ages of the Discoveries*. Farnham: Ashgate, 2009.

De Stoppelaar, Johannes Hermanus. *Balthasar de Moucheron: een bladzijde uit de nederlandsche handelsgeschiedenis tijdens den tachtigjarigen oorlog*. The Hague: Martinus Nijhoff, 1901.

Donkersloot-De Vrij, Marijke. *The World on Paper: A Descriptive Catalogue of Carto-graphical Material Published in Amsterdam during the Seventeenth Century*. Amsterdam: Theatrum Orbis Terrarum, 1967.

Hexham, Hendrick. *Het groot woordenboeck gestalt in 't Neder-duytsch, ende in 't Engelsch*. Rotterdam: Arnout Leers, 1648.

Holt, John Clifford. *The Sri Lanka Reader: History, Culture, Politics*. Durham: Duke University Press, 2011.

Liedtke, Walter. *Vermeer and the Delft School*. New Haven: Yale University Press, 2001.

Lynam, Edward. 'Floris Balthasar, Dutch Map-maker, and his Sons'. *The Geographical Journal* 67, no.2 (1926): 158–61.

Manzano Baena, Laura. *Conflicting Words: The Peace Treaty of Münster (1648) and the Political Culture of the Dutch Republic and the Spanish Monarchy.* Leuven: Leuven University Press, 2011.

Muller, Frederik. *Catalogue of Books and Pamphlets, Atlases, Maps, Plates, and Autographes Relating to North and South America, Including the Collections of Voyages by de Bry, Hulsius, Hartgers, etc.* Amsterdam: Frederick Muller & Co., 1877.

Spies, Marijke. *Arctic Routes to Fabled Lands: Olivier Brunel and the Passage to China and Cathay in the Sixteenth Century.* Amsterdam: Amsterdam University Press, 1997.

Van den Brink, P. 'De kaart van Rijnland door Floris Balthasar van Berckenrode'. In *Prins Maurits' kaart van Rijnland, en omliggend gebied door Floris Balthasar en zijn zoon Balthasar Florisz. Van Berckenrode in 1616 getekend*, edited by K. Zandvliet, 1-16. Alphen aan den Rijn: Canaletto, 1989.

Van Groesen, Michiel. *The Representations of the Overseas World in the De Bry collection of Voyage (1590-1634).* Leiden and Boston: Brill, 2008.

Van Hooijdonk, Eva. 'News Propaganda and Poetry: Language and Imagery in Hugo Grotius's Maurice Epigrams'. In *Dynamics of Neo-Latin and the Vernacular: Language and Poetics, Translation and Transfer*, edited by T. Deneire, 136-62. Leiden: Brill, 2014.

Van Spilbergen, Joris. *Journal of Spilbergen: The First Dutch Envoy to Ceylon 1602.* Translated by K. D. Paranavitana. Sri Lanka: s.n., 1997.

Van Spilbergen, J. *'T Historiael journael van tghene ghepasseert is van weghen drie schepen, ghenaemt den Ram, Schaep ende t' Lam: ghevaren wt Zeelant vander stadt Camp-Vere, naer d'Oost- Indien, onder tbeleyt van Joris van Speilberghen generael, anno 1601. den 5. Mey, tot in t'eylant Celon, vervatende veel schoone geschiedenissen, die by haer op dese reyse gheschiedt zijn, inden tijdt van twee jaer elff maenden, neghentien daghen.* Delft: Floris Balthasar, 1605.

Zandvliet, K. 'Kartografie, Prins Maurits en de Van Berckenrodes'. In *Prins Maurits' kaart van Rijnland en omliggend gebied door Floris Balthasar en zijn zoon Balthasar Florisz. Van Berckenrode in 1616 getekend,* edited by K. Zandvliet, 17-50. Alphen aan den Rijn: Canaletto, 1989.

Zandvliet, K. *Mapping for Money: Maps, Plans and Topographic Paintings and Their Role in Dutch Overseas Expansion During the 16th and 17th Centuries.* Amsterdam: Batavian Lion International, 1998.

A Response to Danielle Gravon

Yolande Hobbs

I want to play the devil's advocate a bit by suggesting an opposing view on why De Bry might have edited the journal in the way he did. Although I'm not an expert, I'm going to make a case that instead of seeing this as a negative thing, De Bry was actually trying to protect Dutch heritage and not change it. I'm going to start by asking whether De Bry had the right to neutralise polemic language in Spilbergen's travel account.

As Danielle mentioned in her speech, by changing the language and images in *t' Historiael Journael,* De Bry played a part in changing Dutch heritage. But can you interfere with your own cultural heritage? Or can we look at this in another way? I want to evaluate this from both a textual and then an iconographical standpoint. I will start by looking at the text.

De Bry was a Protestant who fled the Spanish Inquisition because of his views on religion.[1] He was a Dutch Protestant like Spilbergen and therefore, would have had the same or a very similar cultural heritage. As I have learnt from the course 'The Global Artefact' at UCR, cultural heritage is not like a switch, as it is almost impossible to turn off. This can be seen in the fact that De Bry did not remove all of the anti-Catholic elements from the text of his edition, but rather altered them. Therefore, as said previously, I would like to suggest that De Bry focused more on promoting Dutch Protestant ideals in countries that were Catholic than on interfering with Dutch heritage.

In modern terms, Spilbergen's account would be seen as hate speech criticising both Buddhism and Catholicism. Just as with

---

[1] van Groesen, *Representations*, 2.

hate speech today, this account would not have gone down well with the people who felt targeted by Spilbergen. Therefore, this version of the journal would have been banned in Catholic countries and would have never been translated into Latin, for example. Therefore, De Bry's amendments made it possible for the account to still be read outside the Protestant world. However, there are small hints of Protestant propaganda which remain subliminally in the text. These hints promote to Catholic readers that Protestantism is the superior religion, therefore, expanding and imposing the Protestant ideology. If this theory would be accepted, we could say that De Bry did not amend the text to suit a confessionally divided readership, but to subliminally challenge the Catholic faith.

However, does this theory work in terms of the images? Did De Bry edit the account in the way he did, by removing the coat of arms, to try and promote the Protestant faith through images? Probably not, because Protestants were trying to get away from religious images. Therefore, if it was not to promote religion, why would De Bry remove the coat of arms? Moreover, can we still relate this concept back to De Bry trying to protect Dutch heritage? I think we can.

The images used in the account were siege maps and coats of arms which are usually pro-Republic propaganda. Therefore it can be argued that the Zeeland coat of arms on the map showed pro-Republic propaganda in a time of unrest, the Eighty Years' War. Maybe he thought that foreign readers might view the coat of arms in a different way, which could be wrongly taken out of context. It might re-enforce the idea of the Eighty Years' War into foreign readers' minds, making the Netherlands seem weak and divided. Who would want such an image for their country? Bringing this concept into the present, we can observe a similar thing happening in Britain. Brexit has divided the British population, but when presenting themselves to Brussels, British politicians still try and show a united front. Thus, maybe De Bry was just doing the same as the Prime Minister of the UK is doing now.

With these two examples, you could build a case that De Bry was trying to protect and promote Dutch culture abroad. However, it does put into question why his edition became more popular in the Netherlands. The fact that his work eclipsed Spilbergen's is interesting, as it hides a part of Dutch history from the Dutch population. Therefore, we should ask why De Bry's edition was more popular. And for this, I think we need to ask: At what point does something become historical or cultural heritage?

Eighty years is a long time for a war to last, and maybe the Dutch population got bored with reading and seeing politically loaded propaganda. Just like people in the UK try to look for objective versions of what is happening with Brexit, seventeenth-century Dutch readers might have found De Bry's edition more objective. Moreover, because the Dutch readers were living through the war, they did not view it as historical-cultural heritage but, were familiar with the facts. Throughout the war, his edition was popular and when the war ended, his edition was still preferred.[2] However, the war could also be seen as historical-cultural heritage, as it had begun so long ago. These circumstances perhaps caused a disconnect between the Dutch public of the day and what they saw as their historical and cultural heritage. If this is the case, you cannot really accuse the Dutch population of preferring a cleaned-up version.

Simplified, it's like saying that because someone is British they should be reading extremely pro-Brexit or Remainder propaganda to make it popular because one day Brexit will be part of British historical heritage and will be looked back upon. Therefore, if objective sources are favoured over extremist Brexit or Remainder

---

[2] Gravon, 'Kandy', 55.

propaganda and read more, in the future, these sources would be seen as having concealed a part of British history. But is this vision really true? Or will it just conceal a really biased part of British historical cultural heritage with ideals only held by a few?

To come back to De Bry, I would like to finish by saying that though he did smooth over Spilbergen's version and eclipsed it, it can be argued that his version was more popular amongst the Dutch because it was more objective. However, our 21st-century views may perceive the historical and cultural heritage side of this account to be more important than they might have been. It also could be argued that De Bry might have changed the account to protect and promote the Dutch identity abroad by subtly pushing Protestant propaganda and showing a unified front.

References

Gravon, Danielle. ''Kandy is Now Flanders': Mapping Dutch Identity in the First Dutch Envoy to Ceylon'. *Bulletin of the John Rylands Library* 95, no. 2 (2019): 43-62.

Van Groesen, Michiel. 'The De Bry Collection of Voyages (1590-1634): Early America Reconsidered'. *Journal of Early Modern History* 12, no. 1 (2008): 1-24.

Van Groesen, Michiel. *The Representations of the Overseas World in the De Bry Collection of Voyages (1590-1634)*. Leiden: Brill, 2008.

'Ask Granny How to Sew, Lad'
Recycling Intangible Heritage for Sustainability[1]

Vicki Haverkate-Emmerson

When staring at an uncertain future defined by climate change it is hard not to be scared. In fear, human beings can feel paralysed and unable to act. And yet, act we must. We must all *do something* to reduce our personal and collective impact on the planet, and we need to do it fast. The problem is that we also don't know what to do for the best. In the global north, a standard response to a problem is to buy something to fix it. Or, if nothing suitable exists, we might try to create a new product. Perhaps other people will buy that. Thus, it is not surprising that a whole industry has developed around so-called 'sustainable products'. According to the marketing, these goods are helping the planet. Often they also profess to be beneficial to some other, usually a community in the global south.

There are two major problems with this approach. Firstly, it is really just a new consumerism. The global north must use fewer, not just different, resources. Cynicism about buying more, however ethically or sustainably sourced, grows. More anxiety sets in. More inaction. Fear and self-efficacy enter an inverse relationship. How can the cycle be broken for the sake of our mental health and ultimately the planet? I want to suggest that perhaps the way forward is to look to the past, particularly to its foodways and to the making and repairing of material culture. To distinguish these traditions and skills from other aspects of traditional culture, and to highlight that they can have impact well beyond the domestic sphere from which they originate, I use the term 'inherited intangible heritage'. Although slightly tautological, I use inherited heritage to mean:

---

[1] This contribution was added at a later stage to the volume, but was based on discussions held on the day.

given to us by our own families and the communities we currently live in and their antecedents. Focusing on heritage we already have, 'recycling', could avoid the second problem. Which is that if we are not careful about whose heritage we use and which goals we ask it to serve, we run the risk of further exacerbating both climate change and the inequalities of the post-colonial and gendered world.

Heritage, Health, and Sustainability

Heritage is good for our mental health. Familiarising ourselves with expressions of our own culture(s), both tangible and intangible, helps us feel better situated in our inherited identities.[2] The effect is seen with various types of physical heritage, historic landscapes, and artifacts.[3] Similarly, intangible heritage like traditional performing arts, rituals, festivities, and crafts involve group activities or mindful activities. Both of these boost mood and confidence.[4] Indeed the current public health crisis seems to have sparked a revival in craft for this reason.[5] Thus heritage could free us from our frozen state so that we can take steps towards reducing our impact on the planet.

In the corner of my bedroom there is a pile of clothes waiting for me to take them to my mother to be repaired or altered. I have amassed various skills in four decades as an archaeologist, educator, and mother but when it comes to making or repairing clothing I don't get much beyond replacing a button. With a mother who can whip up a dress or a pair of curtains with ease and a grandmother who was a prolific and talented knitter I had every opportunity to learn these skills. In the current COVID-19 pandemic, unable to see my mum and spending more time

---

[2] I use the term inherited identities to mean identities we have acquired by accident of birth and upbringing. For example: culture(s), gender, ethnicity, nationality, class, or sexuality.
[3] Darvill et al., *Historic Landscapes*.
[4] Mind, 'How to Improve Your Mental Wellbeing'.
[5] Suri, 'Not a Crafter?'.

looking at it, the pile has set me thinking. Without access to my mother's skills I would have little choice but to waste and consume more. What other opportunities to gather sustainable knowledge and skills from our ancestors do we overlook and why? When it comes to clothing, there is little incentive to repair. The shift in clothing production to the global south combined with increasing mechanisation means that new items can be found at astonishingly low prices.[6] Whilst we may well be aware of the environmental impact or the human impact of these cheap clothes, we do not always have the financial means or the willpower to resist such prices.[7] Should we be wealthy and concerned enough to insist on clothing that is less damaging to the planet or its producer we are still at risk of 'greenwashing'.[8] Not only are businesses regularly misleading us about the extent to which our purchasing is really sustainable, we are of course misleading ourselves.[9] Repairing clothing is always more sustainable than replacing it, the same applies to many other products. We simply need to use less.

The pandemic also led our family to hit on an idea to be outside and active in a socially distant way. We'd get an allotment. I was surprised that there were plenty vacant locally and with a little trial and error and some tips from our allotment neighbours we discovered how to grow a surprising abundance of vegetables. I thought of my grandfather and his tomatoes. Great for our wellbeing. However,

---

[6] Lu, *The Future*.
[7] An environmental impact, e.g. the draining of the Aral Sea for cotton production; human impact, for instance, the collapse of the Rana Plaza factory complex in Bangladesh in 2013.
[8] Terra Choice, 'Green Washing Report'.
[9] Canadian marketing consultancy Terra Choice (now acquired by UL) identified seven sins, misleading environmental claims. 1. The trade off (highlighting one environmentally friendly aspect of a product but omitting to explain the damaging aspects). 2. Lack of proof. 3. Vague descriptions. 4. False endorsements by environmental brands. 5. Irrelevance (such as stating the product is free from a substance that is banned anyway). 6. Promoting the product as the lesser two evils. 7. Lies.

when I occasionally discovered a fragment of pottery or brick which likely came from the dumping of rubble after heavy damage to the town centre in 1940, I was aware that for his generation these skills had meant much more.[10] This thought, combined with the worsening pandemic, begged the question: How many communities globally would be able to survive using only local resources if necessary? Foodways were one aspect of intangible heritage I always thought I had seized upon. Nonetheless, this was the first time I'd grown my own food. My grandmother was a wartime recipe writer and an excellent home cook and my mother and I have kept her skills (and even her sticky handwritten recipe books) alive in our own kitchens.

However, as the lockdown found me restricting myself to a single weekly shop and as more vegetables than we could eat or give away sprung from the allotment, I realised something. I could cook, but I did not really understand my food as my grandparents had done. I had never really thought about the best way to store food until I was faced with a courgette mountain. Once I engaged with the question, the knowledge to store and preserve was very easy to find.[11] I used to think that I was avoiding waste by only buying the food I needed every few days. Now I realise at a glance that shops often do not store fresh fruit and vegetables well.[12] Therefore rotten ones just end up in their bin, not mine.[13] Now my weekly haul all stays fresh. So here we have accessible knowledge that requires almost no skill to act, doesn't involve buying a new product, and reduces waste. Perhaps it is not too late for me to learn how to sew either.

---

[10] We live in Middelburg in the south of the Netherlands. A combination of bomb damage and a fire caused by Allied anti-aircraft guns in May 1940 destroyed much of the medieval town centre and the rubble was dumped where our allotment is today.
[11] An internet search was all that was needed.
[12] Never mind the obvious evils of plastic packaging.
[13] To share with you just one example: Keep a wet cloth or paper towel on the bottom of your broccoli and dry one on the top and it lasts far, far longer.

Why we need a decolonial framework of knowledge

Heritage is also knowledge. It has been noted that there is much knowledge to be harnessed from our own genetic and geographical ancestors, but this of course applies beyond that sphere. By investigating global epistemologies we may yet *discover* knowledge that could be employed to benefit the planet. Brown and Sprague discuss interesting examples of how *indigenous* knowledge might be used in the following chapter. Rather like the argument that the cure for cancer is waiting in the Amazon, it could be argued that we must preserve all knowledge, just in case! Whilst creating such a knowledge bank seems a noble endeavour, I will explain that it can potentially be damaging if practices of consumerism and (gendered) coloniality are not avoided.

A key tenet of sustainability is to reuse and recycle what we already have to hand. We can apply this to knowledge of intangible heritage too. A useful concept is to think of cultivating our existing knowledge.[14] Rutazibwa argues that first we must de-mythologize our goals. What do we want knowledge to do for us? We should also ask: How was the problem caused? And, what are the myths blocking our pathway out?[15] It's easy to state that what caused climate change is living beyond the means of our planet. But, the myth we need to debunk here is that this is a global truth. Most people on Earth live well within its means.[16] Part of the problem is that those who do not have been exploiting such sustainable communities for centuries, to the detriment of both peoples and natural environments. So, is the goal of the world's over-consumers *really* to live within the means of the planet? Or just to maintain their/our lifestyles without feeling guilty? The latter is not going to help reduce climate change. Importantly, it is

---

[14] Rutazibwa, 'On Babies and Bathwater'.
[15] Ibid.
[16] Esteva, *The Future of Development*.

also not possible to achieve the former by repeating the behaviours that are causing the problem.

Rutazibwa argues that once we have identified and de-mythologised a problem we should identify experts to help address it. We should de-silence those experts whose voices have been ignored. In the case of *the pile*, the expert is my mother. Sorry for ignoring your knowledge, Mum! This may sound flippant but it leads to a serious point. If we wish to include the voices of silenced experts we should look to our own communities. Whilst we may be drawn to thinking about domestic crafts in the global south, whose makers are so often marginalised, looking to 'discover' new, *exotic* crafts or skills is rooted in both consumerism and coloniality. It is also deeply gendered, as I will explain in the following section. But first an example.

The COVID-19 situation and the disappearance of tourists in East Africa has left pastoralist groups across the Rift Valley dependent on food aid. This in spite of a year of near perfect natural conditions for their inherited foodways. There is a deep irony and tragedy around the way in which mass tourism's hunger for cultural heritage, including craft products, and for environmental sustainability as manifested by the protection of wildlife and landscapes, has led to once perfectly sustainable communities becoming dependent on tourists arriving by carbon-pumping flights, and in time losing traditional skills and resilience.[17] Interest in specific aspects of heritage alone may lead to what we might call cultural cash crops and a resulting over-exploitation of resources.[18] This is followed by increased dependence on consumerist systems to the detriment of a society's cultural heritage as a whole, and even

---

[17] Ogada, 'What Chinese People Eat'.
[18] DeMotts (2017) discusses baskets which are hugely popular with tourists to Botswana. Interestingly male community leaders feel that making the baskets has become unsustainable but the female makers argue the natural resources are still sufficient. The truth is unclear but changes to local economies, (gendered) power structures, and environments are evident.

epistemicide.[19] It is far more desirable to *cultivate* the knowledge that was 'always there, to be unearthed and bound back differently, by anyone into knowledges'.[20] Vásquez suggests that we might put north-south encounters on hold until we can conduct them in a more equitable way.[21] I have also argued elsewhere that focusing locally helps us address global issues more successfully.[22] The current global pandemic may just give us the space to re-evaluate.

Why we need a feminist framework of action

Cultivating our inherited knowledge of domestic skills in the global north might contribute to sustainability. But who exactly should take up this task? Despite my emphasis on my own experience with *the pile* and on my mother and grandmother, I am by no means advocating that the lion's share of this effort should fall to women. Nor is my cis-gender, heterosexual experience intended to be read as normative. Events of recent years, not least the COVID-19 pandemic, have exposed the fact that we cannot be complacent about the achievements of feminism. They may be fragile. Even in nations with high levels of gender equality, families spending more time at home have shown increases in the burden of household tasks for women but not men.[23] As this is coupled with an economic uncertainty that also disproportionately impacts part-time or less senior workers (women), the yoke of financial responsibility for families fits all too easily back onto the shoulders of men. There are also practical reasons to press this point. Middle-aged, educated (middle-income) women, have less leisure time than their male or less-educated counterparts: the fewest 'hours off' of all working -age adults (at least in the Netherlands).[24] Traditional skills might

---

[19] Ogada, 'What Chinese People Eat'.
[20] Rutazibwa, 'On Babies and Bathwater'.
[21] Vásquez, 'Decolonial Practices'.
[22] Friedman, Haverkate et al., *Going Glocal*.
[23] Fergusson, 'I Feel Like a Fifties Housewife'.
[24] Roeters, 'Leisure'.

be able to increase sustainability in our lifestyles but the potential is diminished if we hang on to sexist and classist ideas of who should practice them.

So how to ensure that everyone, regardless of gender, has the self-efficacy to recycle their inherited domestic tool kit? Current concepts of what constitutes domestic labour, and the damaging gendered divisions of it, are actually fairly recent constructs. Before the *long nineteenth century* (1797-1914), it was standard for material culture to be either created in the home or by artisans.[25] Whilst there might have been predictable gendered patterns in which tasks fell to whom, stigmas attached to individuals who did not conform to this were yet to take hold.[26] Take the rather striking example of King Henry VIII's enjoyment of embroidery.[27] Much of the idea that men's labour should be embodied and generate capital is a product of the Industrial Revolution.[28] It was only then that 'male' material culture production and indeed men themselves were largely removed from the home. The resulting development was of toxic attitudes surrounding men doing work that was unlikely to cause either any physical strain or lead to monetary gain; 'women's work' is also rooted in that time. Pre-nineteenth-century concepts of masculinity in Europe were more defined by honour and poise than taciturn physical toughness.[29] Giving further strength to the call to men to ignore stereotypes and take up the needle is a look at an environment in which one might expect men to adhere very

---

[25] Gowerly, 'Making Masculinity'.
[26] Ibid.
[27] Charles de Marillac, Ambassador of France noted in 1539: '*The King [...] now gives himself up to amusement, going to play every night upon the Thames, with harps, chanters and all kind of music and pastime. He evidently delights now in painting and embroidery, having sent men to France, Flanders, Italy and elsewhere for masters of this art, and also for musicians and other ministers of pastime.*'
[28] Gowerly, 'Making Masculinity'.
[29] Ibid; see also Kwame Anthony Appiah's discussion of the decline of the honour code in *The Honor Code*.

strongly to nineteenth-century models of masculinity: the soldiers of the Crimean war. Soldiers, of course, were used to repairing uniforms (the soldiers' sewing kit, named a housewife or *hussif,* dates back to at least the mid-eighteenth century). What is perhaps more surprising is that even in the 1850s, injured soldiers were being taught to sew for therapeutic and creative purposes.[30] Not only was no stigma attached to this but soldiers even won praise from Queen Victoria herself for the quality of their work.[31]

It was also the industrial revolution that saw the growth of a class division between those who made and repaired domestic material culture and the consumers of it.[32] Henry VIII took up embroidery after the death of his third wife, Jane Seymour, whose skills in the craft were renowned. The status of craft itself has declined under industrialisation, though it has seen periods of revival.[33] Indeed, the current pandemic may well spark another one. During the nineteenth century, crafting for leisure or as we might see it, *mindfulness*, remained important to the wealthy. This included men to some extent.[34] But the making and repairing of material culture for daily use, especially lower quality items, became the realm of the poor. Clothing in particular is an important case in point. Quick repairs and the production of lower quality items, or what was known as *slop work*, gradually moved from being small-scale domestic work for poor European women to the global south. This term, from which the phrase 'sloppy' is derived, reflects the way that the skills needed to sustain daily life were becoming outsourced and devalued.[35]

---

[30] Furneaux, *Military Men.*
[31] Ibid.
[32] McBrinn, 'Male Trouble', 27-29.
[33] Such as the late 19th-century arts and crafts movement and the 1960s hippie movement.
[34] McBrinn, 'Male Trouble', 27-29.
[35] Ibid.

During the Second World War, necessity saw a revival in these skills themselves, but only as a hiatus in their depreciation in value. The extreme scarcity of resources, strict rationing, and an organised, collective, goal-driven effort during the forties and fifties meant that, regardless of gender, people found ingenious ways to cultivate all sorts of domestic knowledge old and new.[36] Our sustainability goals would be well served by coaxing this generation's knowledge back to life whilst we can. The war eroded nineteenth-century gender roles too. Women took on farming and factory roles and men learned many a canny repair trick including conscripts learning to use a 'hussif'. But, with so many men on the front, the responsibility to 'make do and mend' at home almost entirely fell on women.

In the second half of the last century, the domestic labour of both men and women became increasingly devalued in the global north. I offer only the briefest outline of this as reasons for it were extremely complex. The process was gendered but factors overlapped reflecting the more flexible social constructs of gender emerging at the time.[37] The 1950s housewife was not just glorified because she was particularly skilled, but also to oust her from the post-war workplace. As more women entered the workforce in the second wave of feminism, women found identities beyond their domestic roles. In addition, once many items became inexpensive or more convenient to replace than to repair, the incentive to invest time or value in these skills was lost. What consequences for human health and indeed the environment might have been avoided if the skill of the frugal home cook and needle worker, both more likely to be female and working or lower middle-class, had been more valued by capitalism and neo-liberalism? Can we bring those skills back, embraced by all, for the sake of the environment?

---

[36] Ginn, Goodman, and Langlands, *Wartime Farm*.
[37] Maxwell and Shields, *Legacy*.

There is indeed some evidence that this could happen in the *sewist* movement. The gender neutral term is used by online groups promoting '#vintagestylenotvintagevalues'.[38] The tens of thousands of Instagram followers of stylist turned sewist Norris Danta Ford, who learnt his skills as a child in order to impress potential foster parents with a smart image, and of Michael Gardiner, also a member of Black Makers Matter, who demonstrates what should really be obvious.[39] Older white women, the Grannies of my title, are not the only ones living close by with knowledge to share. Moreover, they are literally the influencers of more people, regardless of gender, race, or background, taking up the challenge. Equally, the making and repairing of things at home, that was largely done by men in the last century has also been replaced by mass production and globalisation.

Skills to 'forge, carve, weave, mould, (or) ignite' rebranded recently by Peter Ginn not as men's crafts but as 'Slow Tech' are indeed in need of such a conscious re-launch.[40] Conducting what my father called 'little jobs', minor repairs of anything and everything from a toaster to a lawnmower and achieved with bits of wood, solder, or spare fuses is also on the wane. In an infuriating cycle of waste and marketing, many products are built to break or to be impossible to fix at home.[41] The addition of electronics to previously simple mechanical items is responsible for planned obsolescence. In contrast, some manufacturers seem to buck the trend with programmes of repair for their own products, for example: outdoor clothing makers Patagonia's *repair is a radical act* campaign.[42] They must maintain the myth that, as Patagonia's

---

[38] Steinkopf-Frank, 'More Men'.
[39] Ibid.
[40] Ginn, *Slow Tech*.
[41] Utterdahl, 'Planned Obsolescence'.
[42] Repair is a radical act is the marketing campaign of the Patagonia clothing brand. See their website: https://www.patagonia.com/stories/repair-is-a-radical-act/story-17637.html.

CEO states, 'the act of buying itself isn't the problem'.[43] I would most strongly disagree. We need sustainable skills and actions, but *sustainable consumerism* is an oxymoron. Perhaps we should think about whether we really need an item in the first place. Why buy a kettle to replace it every five years? Why not spend an afternoon fixing it? We could buy an expensive, high-quality, lifetime guaranteed kettle. Or we could boil water in a pan.[44] The challenge of looking at our domestic lives with fresh eyes should fall equally to all. Repair as a sustainable act, and craft as a route to mindfulness may be an easier message to spread.

Conclusion

In recent months we have been forced into a smaller spheres, primarily our own homes. Spending time in mine has made me keener to advocate that we reconnect with the domestic skills that form an important part of intangible heritage, like foodways and making and repairing material culture. Doing so is not only sustainable, it can be mindful and leave us mentally more able to act. Moreover, if we choose the (intangible) heritage we have inherited, it is easier to create a decolonial and feminist framework and avoid the exploitation of people who did not contribute to the threat of climate change in the first place.

---

[43] Marcario, 'Repair'.
[44] With a lid on for fuel efficiency.

References

Appiah, Kwame Anthony. *The Honour Code: How Moral Revolutions Happen*. New York: Norton and Company, 2010.

Darvill, Timothy, Kerry Barras, Laura Drysdale, Vanessa Heaslip, and Yvette Staelens, eds. *Historic Landscapes and Mental Wellbeing*. Oxford: Archaeopress Books, 2019.

DeMotts, Rachel. 'Weaving a Living: Gender, Craft, and Sustainable Resource Use in Botswana'. *Journal of Political Ecology* 24 (2017): 368-85.

Esteva, Gustavo, Salvatore J. Babones, and Philipp Babcicky. *The Future of Development. A Radical Manifesto*. Bristol: Policy Press, 2013.

Fergusson, Donna. ''I Feel like a Fifties Housewife': How Lockdown has Exposed the Gender Divide'. *The Guardian*, May 3, 2020. https://www. theguardian.com/world/2020/may/03/i-feel-like-a-1950s-housewife-how-lockdown-has-exposed-the-gender-divide?CMP=Share_iOSApp_Other&fbclid=IwAR2HYADlkljIC6znbDi8QUcBccL0m5b_HDkmMXery5Xkvygfcw0wxI1VHLk.

Friedman, John, Vicki Haverkate, Barbara Oomen, Eri Park, and Marcin Sklad, eds. *Going Glocal in Higher Education: The Theory, Teaching and Measurement of Global Citizenship*. Middelburg: University College Roosevelt and The Drukkerij, 2015.

Furneaux, Holly. *Military Men of Feeling: Emotion Touch and Masculinity in the Crimean War*. Oxford: Oxford University Press, 2016.

Ginn, Peter, Ruth Goodman, and Alexander Langlands. *Wartime Farm*. London: BBC Books, 2012.

Ginn, Peter. *Slow Tech. The Perfect Antidote to Today's Digital World*. Sparkford: Haynes Publishing, 2019.

Gowerley, Freya. 'Making Masculinity: Craft, Gender and Material Production in the Long Nineteenth Century'. *Nineteenth-Century Gender Studies* 14, no 2 (Fall 2018).

Lu, Sheng. 'The Future of Made in China: Robots are Taking over China's Factory Floors'. Accessed December 12, 2020. https://shenglufashion. com/2015/11/29/the-future-of-made-in-china-robots-are-taking-over-chinas-factory-floors/.

Marillac, C. to Montmerency, 1539. Letters and Papers Foreign and Domestic. Henry VIII Vol 14 Part 1 June 1539, 6-10 item 1092. Add. MS, 33,514,f.22. British Museum. https://web.archive.org/web/20111004155140/http://www.royal-needlework.org.uk/content/129/henry_viii_embroiderer_king.

Marcario, Rose. 'Repair is a Radical Act'. Patagonia. Accessed Septermber 30, 2020. https://www.patagonia.com/stories/repair-is-a-radical-act/story-17637.html.

Maxwell, Angie, and Todd Shields. *The Legacy of Second-Wave Feminism in American Politics* London: Palgrave MacMillan, 2018.

McBrinn, Joseph. "Male Trouble': Sewing, Amateurism and Gender'. Paper presented in the 'Post-disciplinarity and Sloppy Craft' session at the *UAAC*, National Gallery of Canada, Ottawa and Carleton University, Canada, October 27-29, 2011.

Mind. 'How to Improve your Mental Wellbeing'. Accessed January 17, 2019. https://www.mind.org.uk/information-support/tips-for-everyday-living/wellbeing.

Ogada, Mordecai. 'What Chinese People Eat'. *Africa is a County*. Accessed October 2, 2020. https://africasacountry.com/2020/09/what-chinese-people-eat?fbclid=IwAR2LsV9qZRbFbsfRgL_W0b3U8aFV92gFGt8ACXJ3bKyJOvzppkv8UhUgMNk.

Roeters. Anne. 'Leisure'. *Netherlands Institute for Social Research*, July 31, 2020. https://digitaal.scp.nl/timeuse1/leisure/.

Rutazibwa, Olivia. 'On Babies and Bathwater: Decolonizing International Development Studies'. In *Decolonization and Feminisms in Global Teaching and Learning* edited by Sara de Jong, Rosalba Icaza, and Olivia U. Rutazibwa, 158-80. Oxon: Routledge, 2018.

Steinkopf-Frank, Hannah. 'More Men Reach for Sewing Machines'. *The New York Times*, December 9, 2020. https://www.nytimes.com/2020/12/09/fashion/sewing-patterns.html.

Suri, Charu. 'Not a Crafter? Here's Why You Should Consider Becoming One During the Pandemic'. *The Washington Post*, May 20, 2020. https://www.washingtonpost.com/lifestyle/wellness/home-crafts-coronavirus-pandemic-calm/2020/05/19/9785e11e-9a11-11ea-89fd-28fb313d1886_story.html.

Terra Choice. 'Sins of Greenwashing'. *UL*, 2010. https://www.ul.com/insights/sins-greenwashing.

Utterdahl, Evelina. 'Planned Obsolescence'. *Go Climate*, October 9, 2019. https://www.goclimate.com/blog/planned-obsolescence/.

Vásquez, Rolando. 'Decolonial Practices of Learning'. In *Going Glocal in Higher Education: The Theory, Teaching and Measurement of Global Citizenship* edited by John Friedman, Vicki Haverkate, Barbara Oomen, Eri Park, and Marcin Sklad, 92-102. Middelburg: University College Roosevelt and The Drukkerij, 2015.

The Answers We Already Have

Ash Brown & Anika Sprague

AB: I am sure we have all experienced fear in life – fear of heights, of the dark perhaps, of the unknown, or of being alone. It is a biological instinct that kept our ancestors alive. But in current society, for most of us, our lives are not under threat on a day-to-day basis. So your brain directs this fear in other directions, sometimes in a manner that is detrimental.

When our fear becomes so overwhelming, we are not sure how to react and this is referred to as hyper-paralytic fear.[1] Sometimes when your brain has no solution to a problem it shuts down to protect you from trauma. This reaction can sometimes be induced in individuals considering the impending climate crisis. We are being told that our world is being destroyed, that we can never get the planet that we had back, and this instills in us such a sense of fear and powerlessness. We are facing problems that we as individuals could never solve by ourselves. So we close our eyes and look the other way.

This exemplifies how fear can become detrimental. However, this does not always need to be the case. Sometimes instead of paralysing us, fear can motivate, become a driving force, and inspire change. The line between fear that freezes and fear that motivates is a fine one. Navigating it is a balancing act mediated by knowledge. People need to feel empowered, to know where to exert effort and make a difference. To know how to save the planet we need a better understanding of how it sustains itself and find our place on that shifting equilibrium.

---

[1] Schmidt et al., 'Exploring Human Freeze Responses', 292-304.

211

Instead of discussing the loss of the planet and adding my voice to an already crowded field, I want instead to talk about loss of knowledge. When we destroy homes and force indigenous communities to move, when we dismiss alternative methods of healing and restoration as primitive, and when we refuse to listen to people – we don't deem them as qualified and we take away the knowledge and the heritage they hold most sacred, we are not only hurting them but ourselves. I fundamentally believe that the answers we need to empower us to face the crisis of the earth head-on come from any aspect of life and I was lucky enough to witness this first-hand.

I spent my summer in Mexico. I didn't go there with the intention of solving the global warming crisis and yet I came back with more of an understanding about how to help than I could ever have come up with on my own. In some indigenous communities in Mexico, the people's relationship with the planet is a one of mutualism and symbiosis. This way of life stems from their belief that in hurting the Earth they are hurting themselves, because they are one and the same. This belief impacts every aspect of their lives, whether that be the constant reuse of water, use of ashes to revitalise fields that lie fallow, or simply building a town where everything is accessible on foot. It permeates every part of life.

Now, one may feel that these life choices are simply not applicable in our own lives. Indeed, perhaps the realities of their implementation in the Western world are challenging but the ideology that underpins them is undoubtedly applicable. The ideas of mutual respect and balance are the cornerstones on which all natural relationships are formed. These epistemologies are built on centuries of knowledge, and yet have much more modern ramifications than one might expect. For example, in some Mexican healing rituals the heat preserved by volcanic stones is essential. The indigenous communities that use the stones worked out that if the rocks can maintain a high temperature, they can also maintain a low temperature. So they set these stones at the bottom of their fridges allowing the temperature to remain cold when the power is off overnight. I am not trying to suggest that the solution to the global warming crisis is to go and put stones in your fridge. However, we in the Western world would not think to look to indigenous communities for solutions to power conservation. We often view their way of life as primitive and simplistic in comparison to our 'modern' world. In our certainty that our way of life is the best we impose our lifestyles on others and in so doing dismiss epistemologies that are not our own. In fact, when we distance ourselves from others, when we remove their heritage and ways of remembering, and when we destroy their livelihoods, we are eliminating that which might just save our future.

So maybe the answers won't all come from scientists in white coats, maybe the solutions have already been discovered by voices that are not yet being heard. The voices being lost to time are not only those of communities vastly different from our own. We are also failing to remember and listen to the generations that have come before us. For example, the current generation might go about cleaning the house with numerous chemical sprays and bleaches. All in sterile plastic bottles releasing chemicals that harm the environment. Yet the previous generations, our parents and grandparents, knew that almost anything can be cleaned with hot water, baking soda, and elbow grease.

It is time to take your hands away from your eyes and unblock your ears. Start listening to others and look at all that already exists, because maybe, just maybe in all that knowledge there are the solutions to problems we are just beginning to understand.

AS: Thank you for both for your talks. I had a similar illuminating experience to Ash's in Mexico that I'd like to share. I was in Cozumel over this past break, working with a SCUBA diving school and progressing towards my dream career as a maritime archaeologist. On my first day, we drifted past a coral reef restoration farm and I was instantly filled with questions. I had seen pictures and videos, but this was different – it was much more complex structurally, more so than I ever could've imagined. I did a lot of research as soon as I had surfaced; I had to satisfy the curiosity that consumed me. I found that this particular coral farm was a product of a coral reef conservation program that implemented biorock, an electro-accumulation of minerals dissolved in seawater, or mineral accretion. Mineral accretion technology is a process that applies safe, low voltage electrical currents through seawater, causing dissolved minerals to crystallize on structures, growing into a white limestone similar to that which naturally makes up coral reefs and the white sandy beaches we all know and love.[2] Biorock materials are the only marine construction material in the world that get stronger with age, grow, and are self-repairing.

This struck me as fascinating, but it also made me aware of the harsh reality that set biorock apart from other mediums – durability. Submerged heritage, both natural and cultural, is often beautifully preserved as a result of lack of oxygen and sunlight in the ocean's depths. Its strength is, however, diminishing at a much higher rate with changing acidity and rising temperatures. In addition, we have the potential threat of heritage above sea-level becoming submerged entirely. By 2100, climate change has the power to inundate an estimated 136 sites considered by UNESCO to be cultural and historical treasures.[3] Allow that number to sink in.

---

[2] Global Coral Reef Alliance, 'Biorock'.
[3] Centre, 'Climate Change'.

Earlier, this question was posed: How do we become more efficient in our relationships with each other, the planet, and the systems humanity has built to support those relationships? In response to this, I would like to elaborate on the Gaia hypothesis. According to this hypothesis, the earth is a living network, and we are intertwined with all other life in existence in a self-regulating system. That does not in any form imply that she does not need us. What it does mean is that if we take care of the earth, the earth will take care of us. We can care for our organisms, as they have provided for us in our times of need. We talk about the relationship between us and the planet – if we take too much, the planet will suffer. Once at that point, as we are now, it's important to reduce the harm coming to the earth, allowing life to replenish itself, while doing what we can to help that process. We can be more efficient in our awareness and in our understanding of the deeply rooted consequences of our actions.

I'd also like to respond to what Ash said about hurting the planet and therefore hurting ourselves. This is essentially Newton's third law – for every action there is an equal and opposite reaction. We affect the earth negatively, we are affected negatively; we affect the earth positively, and we are affected positively. You speak of fear, how it can keep you stagnant, blind to possibilities, but it can also be a tremendous motivator. It all depends on your perception, the way you choose to process and react to the events unfolding in front of you. Through the interconnection of epistemology and agency, a passion is born – its power is immeasurable. You talk about the mindset of optimism and connection that leads to progress. If we choose to understand, accept, and truly believe that we can make a difference, there is nothing stopping us from doing just that.

You talk about the role of compassion and the ego – what of ego versus ecological? The ego can be a dangerous thing – authoritative, destructive, unsustainable – a being above all other life forms: separate. Eco, on the other hand, ties us in with the life around us. Ecological isn't just sustainability – it's compassion. It's regenerative, natural, and balanced. We cannot just take responsibility for invention, but also for destruction. We are a part of something much greater than ourselves.

We heard in many talks today that choices are fueled by beliefs and values: these make up your mindset. If we can apply fear in the most optimal and beneficial way and use it as a tool for progress and forward thinking, and apply it with our awareness of the true impact of our mindset – combined with working not just hard, but smart – it will lead us towards a brighter future. It may be intimidating, but all those who think their actions couldn't possibly make a difference: collectively, they do! If we apply ourselves to conservation efforts with the enthusiasm and dedication we bring to invention, expansion, and technological advancement, we can find a solution. If we can perfect the process of low-voltage electrical currents through seawater, causing dissolved minerals to crystallize, practically recreating and reconstructing the natural foundation of coral reefs, we can perfect other conservation processes.

Don't be afraid to start small. The solution isn't to have 7.7 billion people practicing conservation perfectly, it is to have 7.7 billion people practicing it imperfectly – putting in the effort to make a difference is where success is derived. Ask yourself what you can do to make a difference. Use those reusable bags in the back of your pantry. Conserve water. Eat sustainably and be aware of your carbon footprint. Start within. Reprogram your mind: progress over perfection. When it seems like you can't save the planet: Start basic, start small, and start with you.

References

UNESCO. 'Climate Change Threatens UNESCO World Heritage Sites'. April 10, 2007. https://whc.unesco.org/en/news/319.

Global Coral Reef Alliance. 'Biorock - Global Coral Reef Alliance'. Accessed November 2, 2019. http://www.globalcoral.org/biorock-coral-reef-marine-habitat-restoration/.

Schmidt, Norman B., J. Anthony Richey, Michael J. Zvolensky, and Jon K. Maner. 'Exploring Human Freeze Responses to a Threat Stressor'. *Journal of Behavior Therapy and Experimental Psychiatry* 39, no. 3 (2008): 292–304. https://doi.org/10.1016/j.jbtep.2007.08.002.

The Galactic Case for Conservation

Peter Schultz

My full time 'job' right now – like, what I say when people ask me what I do – is running a small ecological non-profit in the High Plains of Minnesota, in the U.S. This little project is called *The Longspur Prairie Fund*. We work on prairies and wetlands, we run educational and community-based programming rooted in the environment of our region, and, most importantly, we help landowners get their property into permanent conservation easements – to restore their land to its natural state, to then protect it for all time.

This work is important to me.

99% (+) of the native prairie in our area – in all of the U.S. – has been either plowed or paved. *There is less than 1% left.* This last sliver is profoundly significant. Inside that 1% are all that remains of an entire ecosystem that once covered millions upon millions of acres. The billions upon billions of birds, flowers, animals, grasses, and insects that once flew, crawled, and thrived across the central plains of the U.S. are gone. Only small and scattered pockets of this vanished ecology remain. We're trying to protect what is left and to help establish more – to push back a little against the cement and steel.

But *why* do this kind of work?

Here, I think it's useful to think about four types of arguments that are commonly deployed by people like me whose work and passion is the protection of our planet and its creatures. While I separate them here for the purpose of analysis, you'll quickly see that all are interdependent to an important degree.

(1) **The religious case for conservation.** There has been an enormous amount of work and research in the last fifty years on the connection between faith and ecology. There is also a great deal of work being done now that seeks to use religion as a practical tool for broadcasting and promoting a conservation ethos. The basic line is this: Creation and the Creator are inseparable. To honor Creation is to honor the Creator, and vice versa. So we get things like this, from the Baha'I faith: 'Nature is God's Will and is God's expression in and through the contingent world', (Tablets of Bahá'u'lláh, p. 142). Or this, from Christian Ecumenical Patriarch Bartholomew a couple of years ago: 'We must treat nature with the same awe and wonder that we reserve for human beings. And we do not need this insight in order to believe in God or to prove his existence. We need it to breathe; we need it for us simply to be'. There are tons more of this kind of thing, of course. American transcendentalists like Ralph Waldo Emmerson, Margaret Fuller, Henry David Thoreau, and Elizabeth Palmer Peabody can also be connected to this type of religious argument.

(2) **The aesthetic case for conservation.** 'Environmental aesthetics' is a relatively new discipline, from the point of view of analytical philosophy. But finding beauty in nature – and seeing that beauty itself as a reason for conservation is an ancient idea. Indeed, while it's not without its problems, aesthetic experience is among the most common starting points for practical environmental ethics. Ask people: 'Why save the Grand Canyon or the Barrier Reef?' and the ready answer will be, 'Because they are beautiful. So grand!' Eugene Hargrove claims that environmental ethics historically started this way, with scenic grandeur, when he writes: 'The ultimate historical foundations of nature preservation are aesthetic'. Recent policy research explores this line in detail: There are, literally, millions of laws across hundreds of nations, that use 'beauty' as the primary reason to protect the Earth.

(3) **The pragmatic/economic case for conservation**. Pragmatic arguments for conservation are a different animal altogether and commonly revolve around so-called 'environmental services'. Here, the argument is rooted in basic survival and the 'life support system' that the Earth provides for us. Without clean air and clean water, we cannot live. Without an ozone layer, we cannot live. Without stable oxygen content, we cannot live. (The list goes on.) In fact, the value of these services has actually been measured. Everything the Earth does for us: The water cycle, the tides, the oxygen cycle, all the various pieces of the Earth's 'life support machine' is worth about $33 trillion a year. Within this line of reasoning, conservation is vital for human survival on a basic, practical, pragmatic level. If we don't care for our own 'life support system', we face radical 'expenses' and, ultimately, the end of our species.

(4) **The ethical/moral case for conservation**. Ethical arguments for conservation are bound up with concepts of human duty and obligation towards other creatures and our shared environment, specifically philosophical ways in which we can extend moral standing to non-human creatures and ecosystems. There are countless ways in which this issue has been approached in terms of philosophical ethics, but perhaps the most fundamental question that must be asked when regarding a particular environmental ethic is simply this: What obligations do we have concerning the natural environment? *If* the answer is simply that we, as human beings, will perish if we do not constrain our actions towards nature, then that ethic is considered to be 'anthropocentric'. Anthropocentrism, of course, literally means 'human-centeredness', and in one sense all ethics must be considered anthropocentric. (After all, as far as we know, only human beings can reason about and reflect upon ethical matters, thus giving all moral debate a definite 'human-centeredness'.) However, within environmental ethics,

anthropocentrism usually means something more than this; it usually refers to an ethical framework that grants 'moral standing' solely to human beings. Thus, an anthropocentric ethic claims that only human beings are morally considerable in their own right, meaning that all the direct moral obligations we possess, including those we have with regard to the environment, are owed *only* to our fellow human beings.

While the history of Western philosophy is dominated by this kind anthropocentrism, it has come under considerable attack from many environmental ethicists in the last fifty years. Such thinkers have claimed that ethics must be extended beyond humanity, and that moral standing should be accorded to the non-human natural world because we are a part of it – and it is a part of us. Some have claimed that this extension should run to sentient animals, others to individual living organisms, and still others to holistic entities such as rivers, species, and ecosystems. Under these ethical arguments, we have obligations in respect to the environment because there exists some kind of equality between all creatures or entities within the environment themselves. For environmental ethicists, almost all environmental arguments for conservation involve extending moral standing to other beings and the living systems of which they are a part.

This brings us to our potentially new idea – the fifth 'type' of argument 'the galactic argument for conservation'. This idea is rooted in a relatively new set of ideas called 'the rare Earth hypothesis'. The 'rare Earth hypothesis' is an idea that came out of trans-disciplinary work in planetary geology, astronomy, and astrobiology. The theory argues that the origin of life and the evolution of biological complexity sophisticated enough to host or engender human intelligence required an improbable combination of astrophysical, climatological, and geological events and circumstances.

According to the hypothesis, complex extraterrestrial life is an outrageously improbable phenomenon and likely to be rare – *extremely rare*. The term 'rare Earth' originates from *Rare Earth: Why Complex Life is Uncommon in the Universe* (2000), a book by Peter Ward, a geologist and paleontologist, and Donald E. Brownlee, an astronomer and astrobiologist, both faculty members at the University of Washington.

Now – for someone like me – who grew up watching *Star Trek* and *Star Wars*, for someone who loves Carl Sagan and Neil deGrasse Tyson, this was a very hard idea even to think about. In other words, I love the idea of aliens. I love the idea of a galaxy filled and teeming with life, waiting to connect with us. It's great. By the same token, coming from the opposite direction of the issue, I'm instinctually resistant to the idea that humans can or should or would start thinking about themselves as the center of the Universe again. Indeed, it took over a millennium to get rid of the geocentric/Ptolemaic model of the Earth and along with it their various attendant, anthropocentric absurdities. Why on Earth would we ever go back to this?

There are some interesting reasons to take a second look at this idea – and that's what I want to do, very briefly.

(Important disclaimer: I'm not suggesting that I'm an expert on the rare Earth hypothesis or that I'm even fully convinced by it. Rather, I think that this set of ideas presents some interesting and interconnected points that can be directly connected to the state and practice of 'boots in the mud' conservation work.)

So, at the root of the rare Earth hypothesis is the idea of 'barriers to life', or 'hurdles to intelligence'. These are not the same thing – not by a long shot – but for the purposes of this little talk, we're going to talk about them like they are.

These 'barriers' are geological, cosmological, astrophysical, astronomical, and climatological 'challenges' that needed to be 'overcome' in order for life to be possible on the planet Earth. Here's the list: (1) The right location of the solar system in the right kind of galaxy; (2) a planet orbiting at the right distance within the solar system from the right type of star; (3) a solar system with the right arrangement of planets; (4) a planet with a continuous and stable orbit; (5) a terrestrial planet of the right size; (6) a planet with plate tectonics; (7) a planet with a magnetosphere; (8) a planet with the perfectly sized moon; (9) a planet with an atmosphere conducive to life; (10) once all those are in place, we also need 'life triggers' to take place at exactly the right time, evolutionarily speaking, and nobody really knows what that is.

Each one of these ten 'hurdles' represents a kind of 'lottery'. In each case, the rare Earth hypothesis argues, we 'won the lottery'. What's truly extraordinary about this is what happens with the mathematics. Even if our lottery odds in each of the ten cases were 1,000 to 1 – much, much worse than any real lottery! actually very good odds! – when we stack up all ten of the 'hurdles', our Earth becomes 1 single chance in 1,000,000,000,000,000,000,000,000,000,000. One chance in a decillion. (Have you ever even seen that word used before?)

You can see where this is going, can't you?

If there is only one planet like this, then all arguments for conservation immediately take on a different kind of pressure, become loaded with a different kind of urgency. While I'm a devoted atheist, religious arguments for conservation (for good or ill) become more forceful for believers. While I think there's more to the Earth than pretty mountains and sunsets, thinking that we might be the only beings able to appreciate the beauty of these phenomena does give pause. There can be little doubt that we need a 'functioning Earth' to live, but how much more 'valuable' are the 'ecological services' provided by our planet when we apply the basic laws of economic scarcity to them? And as for ethics – all morally derived reasoning for the protection of our home punch a decillion times harder when the Earth is considered rare. If the Earth is rare, when we lose an insect, a mammal, a person – we lose something beyond precious, something fundamentally irreplaceable – on a cosmic scale.

Let's conclude with one final idea, something that I hinted at earlier:

One of the objections to the rare Earth hypothesis is not 'scientific' – that is, not geological, astrophysical, or climatological. Rather, this objection is 'conceptual' or 'philosophical', namely, that the rare Earth hypothesis lends support to an *anthropocentric view* of the world, the galaxy, and the universe. If there's only us, then it's all about us. Us, us, us!

This is indeed a problem.

We've worked hard to challenge the idea that humans are the end, the beginning, and the center of everything, to begin to situate ourselves more carefully and realistically within the various matrices of which we are a part. And yet, the idea that we're not at least partially in charge of our planet is clearly false. The idea that our personal decisions don't have direct and meaningful impacts – both individually and collectively – on our distant and immediate surroundings is also clearly false. At the center of human-induced climate change is human action. The whales, the bees, the polar bears aren't destroying our land, our air, and our water. We are.

So – perhaps, in some ways – it's time to start thinking really hard about our own presence and power, *here*, where we live; to reassert our uniquely human agency over our planet, this place, *our place*. Perhaps it's time to 'own' certain comforting, problematic, and terrifying aspects of our unique authority, *here*, where we live.

We might be the only species in the galaxy with a home like this to protect.

A Response to Peter Schultz

Clarissa Frascadore

First, I would like to thank Peter for his speech, as well as the previous speakers as their speeches have been extremely enriching, and fit the same topic I would like to discuss today.

When I first read about the rare Earth theory, I was scared that I would not understand the science behind it. I could understand why conserving and, even more, saving our planet is important. Because of this, I was ready to engage in a discourse about reasoning on why we should conserve our planet. I was prepared for the religious argument and the aesthetic argument, but I was a bit less prepared for the astrophysics argument.

When I first arrived in UCR, I believed I wanted to study science, but soon I realised I was looking at the wrong questions: I was asking 'how did humans evolve'? So I was receiving answers on the complex evolutionary system when I was actually interested in 'which decisions, passions, mistakes did humans make that brought us to where we are now'? Or I was studying 'how is it that we move'? rather than 'what is it that moves us'? So I was receiving answers in biology on bones and muscles when I wanted to know what it is that truly moves us, why we put so much value in objects, and why we feel the need to protect them, for instance. In my first semester I had to admit it was really hard to pose the right questions when I was busier trying to understand which subject and which field they belong to.

When I read about the rare Earth theory, it was clear to me this was going to be one of those situations where the knowledge we have as humans is more needed to solve the issue than the interpretation of which field this answer belongs to. In other words, if we had to fit this theory and the problems and consequences of it in a UCR, or any other university department, it would be quite hard. This is a scientific theory, but we would also need scientists to think of philosophical matters on what this theory means and how to use it for the better. Otherwise, it would die in its theoretical framework, or even worse, bring in dangerous anthropocentric views of the universe. The field of environmental studies would be a good place to start, as we would need the help of social scientists, such as human geography students and scholars, for the realization of a project, as well as practicalities drawn from the study of people's cultures and possibly different ways to apply this knowledge.

We would need someone that explains the theory to people, perhaps through art. We could put this theory in a philosophy class so they could solve the ethical problem. And we could put it in an art class, but art students would need to understand the science behind it and I know that I could not do that fully.

Nowadays, the most pressing problems need to be solved with interdisciplinarity (and this is why liberal arts and science colleges are so important). However, sometimes it is difficult to apply this idea to our own research. As a student, coming from my previous education and influenced by how the academic world is structured, I think of problems as archaeological problems, historical problems, and mathematical problems. In this whole process, sometimes I forget that there is a problem to solve.

If we look at the philosopher Finnis and his theory on the seven basic goods that every human needs to be happy, our planet plays a role in each one of them. The first one is 'life' – we need our planet to stay alive and we need to stay alive to be happy.[1] Another example is aesthetic experience, or religion. As Peter already informed us, they

---

[1] McCarthy, 'A Summary'.

are used among other arguments for the conservation of our planet. A basic need that is particularly interesting to me is knowledge. I think that for this specific audience, this is extremely important because we are all scholars and students and professors and writers and so we base our lives on knowledge. We always want to know more, and now we are in front of the fact that our planet is unique and we need to decide what are we going to do with this knowledge.

Previous speeches already highlighted that we can save the planet through many different fields – with science, art, and many more, such as the one Peter is carrying out. Another good way to go about this would be to find unity among all fields and to find a way in which everyone can feel involved. We already have the tools to save the planet and those tools are partly based on what we study, but I don't think that those are enough.

In the multidisciplinary conference 'Futures of Food' hosted by the RIAS (Roosevelt Institute for American Studies) in Middelburg on 10 and 11 October 2019, different scholars and artists spoke about a number of ongoing projects regarding foodscapes and productivity in the future. One of the focuses of the conference was sustainability in food production. There, a member of the audience, and fellow classmate, expressed her difficulty in researching which foods are good and which are bad for the environment. Asking yourself questions like, 'is it better to buy biological food from the supermarket, local food from the market, or food that does not come in plastic?', is not an uncommon experience. This is mainly caused by the large amount and heterogeneity of information available on these topics, which can result in inaccessibility. To suggest an answer, the conference presented an art project. Today, the answer suggested is the use of science and personal responsibility, so I ask: Why do we not use both?

One of the main problems in the theories of interdisciplinary research is that it is hard for a scholar to have sufficient knowledge in different fields of study to carry out research which branches into many subjects. It is hard to not be overwhelmed by a large number of standpoints. This is why I don't think it is the responsibility of one single scholar to carry out an interdisciplinary project. Instead, it is the responsibility of scholars to cooperate with other scholars, from different disciplines.

One day a professor told me 'archaeologists should not make internet websites', but actually I think they should – with the help of computer scientist to code, the help of artists to make the website pretty, social scientists to make sure it is understandable for anyone, and a linguist and a rhetorician to check the language used. This is how we move forward and solve problems.

If we have a shot at solving the problem of planetary conservation, it is by interdisciplinarity and cooperation. And I think conferences such as this one are extremely necessary for it. If there is one thing I'm bringing home from today's conference, it is that for one reason or another we live in a very unique place and we, as humans, are very unique. And now it is up to us to also be united.

References

Duke, George. 'Finnis on the Authority of Law and the Common Good'. *LEG* 19 (2013): 44.

McCarthy, Hugh. 'A Summary of John Finnis's Theory of Natural Law'. *Hugh McCarthy's ASC Blog* (blog), January 3, 2015. https://hughmccarthylawscienceasc.wordpress.com/2015/01/03/a-summary-of-john-finniss-theory-of-natural-law/.

Omodei, Elisa, Manlio De Domenico, and Alex Arenas. 'Evaluating the Impact of Interdisciplinary Research: A Multilayer Network Approach'. *Network Science* 5, no. 2 (2017): 235-246.

RIAS. 'Conference: Futures of Food'. *Roosevelt Institue for American Studies*, January 23, 2020. https://www.roosevelt.nl/news/conference-futures-food.

Waldman, David Andre. 'Interdisciplinary Research is the Key'. *Frontiers in human neuroscience* 7 (2013): 562.

THE KEYNOTE

MICHAEL STRAND

'BENEVOLENT DISRUPTION'

The following is an edited transcript from the lecture 'Benevolent Disruption' by Michael Strand. The lecture was not presented in a paper format and was conversational and a reflection on the past five years of work dedicated to social practice through craft.

Two textiles, one made and one unmade

Made.

In 2006, my mother was diagnosed with pancreatic cancer. If you know about the disease, it is mainly deadly. And in her case, it would take her life. I spent the last weeks with my mother as a witness to her last days on Earth. This was an incredibly painful process, but I am thankful for the experience of sharing with my mother and learning from her during this time.

In the last week that she was alive, a group of women got together, knitters, and they worked for 48 straight hours to create a prayer shawl for my mother. Every stitch, every movement, they thought about my mother in their own faith tradition and prayed for her comfort. The prayer captured in an object. Every movement in creation was part of imbuing it with love, care, and compassion for somebody that they knew didn't have long on this Earth.

I have been blessed to experience in person some of the greatest works of art in the world. From Picasso's *Guernica* to sacred Temples in Japan, I have been moved by artistic and making mastery. With a lifetime dedicated to the arts, I have never experienced a more powerful moment than when this new sacred object was wrapped around my mother's shoulders. At that moment, I realized the full potential of objects. A final gift of wisdom from my mother. This concept of deeply caring for an object for another human being and the resultant meaning and impact of this object is as old as humanity.

Unmade.

Sonya Clark is a contemporary textile artist in the United States whose work so beautifully challenges many assumptions on many levels and with a textile hammer, unpacks a lot of cultural, racial, and historical issues that face the United States today. In this piece, 'Unraveling and Unraveled', Sonya takes the time as a performance to carefully, and thoughtfully, undo a textile that is a symbol of so much hate and division in our country. And so, as a textile artist, the creation of something is actually a deconstruction and meditation on this [Confederate] flag, and its transformation into three piles of thread – red, white, and blue.

The symbolism of those three colors, combined with the interaction she has with the public while unraveling, thread by thread – unwinding history, not as an erasure but as a community meditation on history, memory, and meaning contained within objects.

So I'm a potter. I love to make things. I went to college not knowing what my future would hold, I had never engaged in art or craft in high school, instead focusing on sports – basketball and football. I started off in psychology and then in my fourth year I took a ceramics class as a general college elective. After three weeks in the class, and understanding the potential of bringing together my mind, body, and heart in making art, I began pursuing a new life in the arts.

While many would say that my work is primarily conceptual and project-based, I am still deeply involved in the craft of making.

There is nothing better than at the end of the day looking back at a hundred objects made, turning out the lights on a day well spent. I was trained to make cups in a way that everything could be the same. Thousands of objects later, I developed a mastery and expertise in making that allows me to be completely nimble in my craft. And after years of exploring form, glaze, content, and selling of objects, I realized I was no longer interested in chasing the next beautiful object.

And so with this realization, I reflected back on the experience I had with my mother and the potential of the object made, and it shifted my perception that instead of focusing on the object as the primary focus of innovation I would look at the spaces between. The space between object and humanity, how we acquire something or how we encounter something, and how the experience can be directly connected to meaning in the object. This is the focus of my creative practice.

I am going to share a few examples of this today and through this hope to inspire you to think differently about the objects around you. First, *The Misfit Cup Liberation Project*. The Misfit Cup Liberation Project is an eight-year-old project that will be completed in two years. Like many of my projects, the genesis of the idea comes from an unexpected experience.

One morning, I was in my kitchen and opened the cabinet that contains my collection of cups. As a potter, my shelves are full of handmade objects from makers around the world. And as I scanned my shelf of cups to select my morning coffee cup I noticed a commercially made, plastic martini glass in the back of the cabinet. It struck me how odd it looked, and that I had not really paid attention to it, even though it was not like anything else in the cabinet. And it suddenly struck me as tragic. That this object would live in some kind of 'cup purgatory'. Never utilized and not thrown away, it existed in this solitary lonely state.

Why was it there? Why don't I use it? Why don't I throw it away? The reason is that it was connected to a moment in time with somebody who was moving away, and during this person's last day in town we had dinner at a Mexican-American restaurant and they were giving away free cups with dinner. So this object is connected to that moment, and ultimately it is a reminder of a dear friend. Through this I imagined millions of these cups scattered across cupboards around the world and I am compelled to 'liberate' them – to get them out of the cupboard and into the world.

The Misfit Cup Liberation Project was born. I have formed an exchange. I create cups that trade for cups that people bring with a story. When they bring in this object, they fill out a form and share this story which is displayed along with their object. Like every experimental project I do, the first iteration is always an unknown. I fear that it may not work, that people may not show up, and that my theory will not be supported by participation. In fact, if I knew what would happen, there would be no reason to actually do the project!

In 2012, at the Plains Art Museum in Fargo we launched the project. I've always been interested in how we engage the public with institutions, which is the reason that when I work with museums, it has to fit into a mission to bring new people to the space. On launch night I did not know what to expect, but a crowd started to form early, and what you might imagine an art opening to be like – people walking carefully, minding space, and sipping wine – is not exactly the response that this exhibition generated. And this is the best image I have for the energy that was created that evening. There is a tradition in the United States called 'Black Friday' which is the first holiday shopping day of the year, and it is notorious for a crush of people and an energy level that is a bit manic. It was a bit like that, without the arguing for queue lines. I had set up a process that was tidy and orderly, and immediately people just started filling out their forms for their cup exchange all over the museum. It was slightly chaotic and wonderful.

Within one hour, all 100 cups that I brought into the museum were replaced by objects and stories brought out of the community's cabinets and into the public view. And this is where the project became really interesting. I really had no idea what people would bring – bad design, strange objects, etc. Instead the focus was intensely on stories, wonderful stories, tragic stories – triumphs, weddings, and divorces. Cups about alcoholism, memories of grandparents, and stolen cups – one on the way to the museum! What I thought might be primarily about interesting objects quickly turned into very compelling and heartfelt stories.

So there is this study that took place a few years ago analyzing the amount of time that people would examine *Mona Lisa*. And in the end, it was something in the order of 10 seconds that people would spend in front of this iconic image. The museum began taking note of the amount of time people would spend with this project and it was over 38 minutes. Reading, considering, examining, and pondering. Histories, stories, and narratives.

One of the most important cups in this first iteration of the project is still an iconic object out of the over 800 I have collected so far around the world. It is titled *Ex-Con*.

> I got this cup in prison. It has my name and inmate number engraved on it. I used it everyday inside

and over three years out of prison. I wanted to exchange it because I want to leave that part of my life behind.

This story accompanied a very non-descript clear/white plastic cup, with an inmate number laser cut into the bottom. This simple story became the focus of the evening.

And there's a buzz, right? And people started gathering around. And he is standing in front of his cup, proud – encircled by a ring of humanity reading the story and considering the strength and importance of that moment. At that moment he became the 'art star', and I comfortably faded into the background and observed and listened. It was at that moment that I knew I would continue this project for the next decade, and I have with the latest version of the Misfit Cup Project taking place in Sweden this past year.

The second iteration of the project took place in Estonia. Again, I did not know what to expect, but the project was part of a very important European exhibition at a major museum. In Estonia they have this television show in the mornings, like the States called 'Good Morning Estonia'. On this show they talked about the project with the curator, who invited the public to bring in these memorable cups. A wonderful elder from an island outside of Tallinn heard about the project and she knew exactly the object she would bring to exchange. The last Soviet-issued cup that she knew of on her island. And so this wonderful 90+ year old woman is escorted from the front of the museum to meet me and exchange the cup in person. This little white cup – industrial and bland – carries so much history. Her story is now archived with the object as part of the growing collection. There were other odd objects: a hair-covered cup, a boot cup, and several erotic cups brought in with stories written in Estonian or Russian, histories captured in this moment connected to objects.

I have been able to do this project in Brazil, Guernsey, Taiwan, Houston, Kansas City, Sweden, the Netherlands, and I even have a single cup from Antarctica. Each culture brings a different perspective, new objects, and interesting heritage perspectives. But what has emerged has also been surprising, although it should not have been. There are significant key themes throughout this collection. Marriage, celebration, loved ones lost, many stolen cups with stories about the theft, and many cups about alcoholism. The range of emotions contained within the objects is remarkable and the consistency of story across cultures manages to connect human culture through the lens of this common every-person object.

In Brazil, the cups are accompanied by much longer stories with the Brazilian storytelling tradition alive in the project where I was told that possibly 'some' of these stories may be more fiction than fact. And in Taiwan, where the process at the largest ceramic museum in the country was organized to the minute and where every participant took a selfie with me and shared the stories and images on social media. In Amsterdam, as part of the Steinbeisser Experimental Gastronomy organization in partnership with a well-known Dutch chef. Each version of the project takes on a local flavor and intensity.

I am now at the later stages of the project with a projected completion date in 2022, ten years after the start, and will be at 1,001 cups, from every continent. Each cup is individually archived, photographed, and digitally documented as part of a cared-for collection. This collection is forming the basis for a book and a major exhibition of all 1,001 cups in the next few years at significant national/ international museums and folk object institutions.

I have learned a great deal from this project, primarily that my role as a maker is that of a facilitator of conversation and storytelling. I create a catalyst through functional objects to connect people through history, objects, and narratives. And in working in this manner I have been able to expand in many directions that gathers stories and narratives, redefining for me the role of making and its connection and value to the public.

Another example of this way of working is the *Bowls Around Town Project*. As a potter, I'm naturally really interested in food and food culture. Specifically, I am curious about food heritage and 'heirloom' recipes and the reasons we have family recipes and traditions. Again, the start of the project comes through a reflection on a unique experience that piqued an interest.

When I was 16 years old my grandmother passed away suddenly. She was 90 years old and very healthy so this was completely unexpected. My grandmother had this tradition of baking black bread – a heavy, sweet rye bread that would accompany any visit, any holiday, and throughout our extended family this was the food version of a 'family crest'. About a month after my grandmother passed away I opened up our deep freezer and noticed a loaf of bread concealed by other items. I quickly realized that this was a single loaf of my grandmother's bread. Now at 16 years old I can only explain my response as something between the greatest Christmas surprise ever and an existential crisis. What do I do? Eat it? Save it? Keep it JUST for me!? The answer was to surprise my family with it, and for one more wonderful morning we sat down with my grandmother through the experience of consuming her bread.

This story, at least on a personal level, has been a guiding moment in my life. Understanding the value of history, and family memory – through this experience – is part of what forms my interest in all of my work today. And this also has led me to inquire with others about their own recipe stories and family traditions.

So with this project I have a handcrafted box, a large serving bowl that I make, a recipe-collecting diary and a camera contained as a package that travels. In a variety of systems, communities, and organizations, variations of this kit have traveled collecting recipes, stories, and images of fellowship with family and friends with these recipes.

This leads to a quick side-note about agency and community. I am very aware of how my presence as the artist, or researcher, has a positive or negative influence on public engagement. What I have learned through this process is that a simple bowl, traveling to and from individuals/families does not have the same cultural baggage that I may bring to the situation. And with that the bowl, as a ubiquitous object – one that needs very little explanation – can move within spaces that I cannot. And so I test where this bowl can travel and circulate.

One of those locations is through fire stations. Fire stations are community centers. Firefighters spend long periods of time together and share meals and living spaces. In the United States there is also a competitive spirit among station houses, competing with another station house. One key component of this process is that in the case of the Portland Fire Department, the bowl travels sequentially through each station house. And each station house can see what the previous stations entered into the book and the images that they took to document the process. And as these images show there is an increase in quality and intensity. It is as if the project grew in capacity and imagination with each fire station's participation. The recipes became more complex and the stories more compelling. (This demonstrated by the images that were included – the images moved from candid photographs to wonderfully designed and composed images.)

This is Brazil, and another partnership with fire stations. Along with stunningly beautiful food and stories, they refused to separate my participation from the work. In true Brazilian fashion they utilized this as an opportunity to have a barbecue and a party – with me as the guest. This is another aspect of my work that I enjoy; I may have 'concepts and internal rules', but ultimately it is set by those I engage, listen to, and serve through the project. Their stories are rich in narrative about how they share space together and have a weekly barbecue that includes family and friends at the fire station. The food – was otherworldly.

Another system of distribution I have worked with is library systems. A library is built to efficiently move information into a community. Their goal is to get people to gather, learn, and check books out. One of the challenges for artists/designers is that there is often a misguided notion that the entire project needs to be invented. There are good examples of artist check-out projects that often fail because there is no sustainable mechanism to continue the project's past initial momentum. And usually these kinds of projects would take place at a museum. As a process, I think of my work as more like an infection agent for good. Why invent a library when you can partner with the library and bring new ideas to a wonderful institution? The museum in this case is irrelevant to the project as its natural home of distribution is the library.

I worked with Curator Namita Gupta Wiggers at the Museum of Contemporary Craft in Portland and met with the Multnomah County Library, which is the public library system in Portland. If you know anything about Portland, it's a wonderfully experimental and alternative city. In our conversations they were saying (casually paraphrased) 'Yeah, we'll try this. But we are not sure anybody's going to really do it, but we'll try it because we're Portland'. So the bowl project went into the library system. So, how effective was this process? The wonderful thing about a library is that the entire process of checkout is an automated system of assessment. On a daily basis we could check to see the progress of the project and whether there was significant participation. After a couple of weeks there was enough demand on the project to have a large waiting list through their system. In fact, it was large enough that the library requested another bowl kit to check out. And over the course of a few weeks about 200 people utilized the process to check the bowl out and share their images and stories.

So the process worked like this: You come into the library and check out the kit. (I am so in love with the idea that my kits actually have library numbers!) You bring the bowl home and unpack and wash the bowl. Carefully fill out the book with information about the recipe, the story behind it, and prepare dinner, with a camera included to document the process. One terrific image from the project looks like a cover to a modern cooking magazine.

What I appreciate about this process and the resulting images is that they are taken through the eye and hand of those participating. It is self-documented. And there is an authenticity in what is shared – the images are important because they come from people who are engaged with it. This aspect of publicly engaged works is vitally important, that the documentation process is not taken from those participating in a colonial manner, but rather is an opportunity to lift up the community voice.

One other extension of the Bowls project was with a partnership with the Southern Catholic Diocese of Brazil. Working with a group of graduate students at the Universidad de Caxias do Sul we met with the Bishop and learned of the tradition of *pequena capel* or little chapel. This is a centuries old tradition of small handheld chapels that church members would check out and bring home to have a bit of the church at home for the week. In talking to the Bishop, who greatly appreciated the concept of the Bowls project, we were given permission to create a new version of this that would be checked out in perpetuity at the church. The idea from our perspective, is that the bowl would become a way for the church community to archive recipes and stories into the church. I imagine a day in the future when I will revisit my friends in Brazil and learn of the stories and images of fellowship within their community. And I imagine 100 years from now when this bowl potentially is still in circulation, adding to the history of information gathered through this simple process.

So what am I working on now – where is this all going?

A couple of years ago I stepped back and examined where exactly in culture do I have agency. Where are the spaces where my learned and lived experiences come together in my own community? In answering this question it is important to understand two really important experiences in my life. One, in 13 years, I have reduced my body weight by about 200 pounds. I have taken the time to slowly, methodically, and carefully focus on my own health. So I have a significant amount of lived and learned experience with health and fitness. Second, on the day before my second son was born in 2004, I made the very specific decision to not consume alcohol. I am a recovering alcoholic of 16 years. I stand tall in recovery and as with many people who have made it onto the other side of addiction, I am both thankful for where I am, and appreciative of the significant lived and learned experience. This leads to where I am at now with making, objects, and memory. So here's a couple of realities about recovery, reinforced by my earlier cup project. So in my cabinet, I had my favorite martini glass. I had my favorite rum and coke glass. I had my favorite everything glass. Cups in my cabinet were constant reminders of the decisions I was making on a daily basis to feed my addiction to alcohol. Think about this for a moment. That which nourishes your body – a cup containing water is also like a weapon of self-harm in the hands of somebody in addiction.

So I work with people who are in recovery. I'm not a psychologist, but I have agency there because one of the roles that many assume in recovery is to help those who are looking to overcome this disease. The process is called 'sponsoring'. I am available for phone calls, help, and encouragement to make the right decision, until the point that the individual can move on without support. So typically this would take place at a coffee shop. So what I have been experimenting with as part of my agency within this system of recovery is instead of meeting at a coffee shop, we meet at the studio. And during our conversation, I make a new cup to replace one of the cups they have in their cabinet. This new cup is now connected, not to me as the maker, but to that moment in conversation where the individual is resolved in their decision to remain sober. It is also made specifically for something healthy to drink: water, lemonade, milk, etc. Now consider that when they open up their cabinet to select their cup, all of the cups that they utilized as part of their addiction have been replaced with new objects as a reminder of their resolve. Individuals in recovery are typically left with a pure intellectual and emotional decision to remain sober. It is a process that is nearly entirely contained within the realm of 'head space'. What if, in addition to this mental and emotional resolve, designed objects became a significant part of recovery? In this case a cup, when held in your hand, provides additional motivation and support to remain sober.

The next step will be to move this to a clinical trial and I am currently narrowing down funding opportunities. Does this mean potters will be a significant partner in helping to solve addiction? That is not even the point – the point is that as a craftsperson, not working in an individual silo, expanding outward and imagining spaces for the arts to exist beyond tradition and examining my own lived and learned experience, I may be of assistance in understanding how design and objects may be part of additional solutions to a pressing issue today.

My pathway as a maker has moved from the tradition of the apprentice model of making, exacting a craft to make exquisite objects of collection. To an organizer of projects that may be more aligned with public history than art. And back to making, but now integrating what I learned as a functional maker and a conceptual artist, with a new practicality that is connected directly to my own lived and learned experience – ultimately working in an area where I have significant community agency. Objects, memory, function, history, and the digital realm come together in my work today. I am now most at ease, existing in a space with no category – with no boundaries and with no limits to where I can move the arts into the world.

www.ingramcontent.com/pod-product-compliance
Lightning Source LLC
Chambersburg PA
CBHW020856270326
41928CB00006B/729